Let Me Be Five

This book offers a step-by-step guide to implementing a play-based curriculum in Year 1 while fully achieving the National Curriculum objectives. The authors explore the key barriers and common pitfalls that often arise around this crucial transition, and show teachers how to successfully lead children from the Reception stage through Year 1 and to the subject-based teaching beyond.

Providing practical advice and guidance for busy teachers, the authors clearly and concisely illustrate their methods with theory, personal stories and colourful photographs from transitional stories they have been a part of. *Let Me Be Five* shows teachers how to plan the curriculum in a way that builds on children's experiences in the Early Years Foundation Stage and gives them meaningful contexts for learning.

Including real-life case studies and views from parents and teachers, this book will give you the knowledge and confidence to plan a play-based curriculum, based on children's interests and developmental needs that will enable every learner to thrive.

Sue Quirk is an advisory headteacher having been a headteacher, an independent consultant and a school improvement adviser in two London boroughs.

Victoria Pettett is head of school of a three-form entry primary school, and the Swale Academies Trust Early Years lead.

The co-authors of this book are senior leaders in a multi-academy trust which includes ten primary schools, in London, Kent and East Sussex.

"In my career I have lost count of the number of school leaders who ask me, 'How can we get it right in Year 1?' This book provides the solution! It comprehensively gives practical advice to set up the learning environment that is essential for a smooth transition from Reception. For the fortunate children who experience this high quality, pedagogically developed, curriculum the rapid progress made in the EYFS will continue into KS1 and beyond. Powerful! Now top of my list of recommendations."
　　　　　*– **Clare Bradley**, Head of School Effra Early Years Centre, formerly EYFS Teaching Consultant, CLLD and phonics lead, London Borough of Lambeth*

"This book provides a wealth of useful and practical advice on how to ensure a smooth and effective transition from Reception into Year 1 and beyond. Written by practitioners for practitioners, it identifies how teachers can plan the Year 1 curriculum in a way that builds successfully on children's experiences in the Early Years Foundation Stage. It is based on first hand evidence of what works best for children across a range of school settings and provides a welcome insight into the current debate on practice in Year 1 classrooms. It is unequivocal in encouraging leaders and teachers to resist the pressure to introduce formal education too early and to ensure that the curriculum is planned to meet the developmental needs of the child."
　　　　　*– **Dr. Pauline Watts**, School Improvement Adviser, former primary headteacher*

"This book supports teachers and senior leaders to understand the pedagogy and beneficial outcomes of reflecting EYFS methods in Key Stage 1, using a progressive play-based approach to learning. Getting transition right is the key to success. Building on what has gone before and providing the right level of challenge through continuous provision in Key Stage 1 provides the right curriculum for all children. This book is an excellent guide for Key Stage 1 teachers who want to present learning-opportunities to children so they can learn in the best way they know. It is a very accessible read with lots of thought-provoking ideas and anecdotes. If you want to be empowered to deliver improved attitudes to learning in Key Stage 1 and to support your pupils to be engaged and excited about their learning, this book is the perfect starting point."
　　　　　*– **Jan Bennett**, former headteacher and lead local authority EYFS adviser*

Let Me Be Five

Implementing a Play-Based Curriculum in Year 1 and Beyond

Sue Quirk and Victoria Pettett

LONDON AND NEW YORK

First edition published 2021
by Routledge
2 Park Square, Milton Park, Abingdon, Oxon, OX14 4RN

and by Routledge
52 Vanderbilt Avenue, New York, NY 10017

Routledge is an imprint of the Taylor & Francis Group, an informa business

© 2021 Sue Quirk and Victoria Pettett

The right of Sue Quirk and Victoria Pettett to be identified as authors of this work has been asserted by them in accordance with sections 77 and 78 of the Copyright, Designs and Patents Act 1988.

All rights reserved. No part of this book may be reprinted or reproduced or utilised in any form or by any electronic, mechanical, or other means, now known or hereafter invented, including photocopying and recording, or in any information storage or retrieval system, without permission in writing from the publishers.

Trademark notice: Product or corporate names may be trademarks or registered trademarks, and are used only for identification and explanation without intent to infringe.

British Library Cataloguing-in-Publication Data
A catalogue record for this book is available from the British Library

Library of Congress Cataloging-in-Publication Data
Title: Let me be five : implementing a play-based curriculum in year 1 and beyond / Sue Quirk and Victoria Pettett.
Description: First edition. | Abingdon, Oxon ; New York, NY : Routledge, 2021. | Includes bibliographical references and index.
Identifiers: LCCN 2020044616 (print) | LCCN 2020044617 (ebook) | ISBN 9780367344191 (hardback) | ISBN 9780367344207 (paperback) | ISBN 9780429325694 (ebook)
Subjects: LCSH: Play. | Early childhood education--Curricula. | Creative activities and seat work. | Active learning.
Classification: LCC LB1139.35.P55 Q57 2021 (print) | LCC LB1139.35.P55 (ebook) | DDC 372.21--dc23
LC record available at https://lccn.loc.gov/2020044616
LC ebook record available at https://lccn.loc.gov/2020044617

ISBN: 978-0-367-34419-1 (hbk)
ISBN: 978-0-367-34420-7 (pbk)
ISBN: 978-0-429-32569-4 (ebk)

Typeset in Bembo
by SPi Global, India
Printed and bound by CPI Group (UK) Ltd, Croydon, CR0 4YY

To Mike Wilson,
whose commitment to high-quality provision has given so many children
a wonderful start to their education and to our husbands, Peter and Chris, for their
support, encouragement and belief in us.

Contents

List of figures	viii
Preface	x
Acknowledgments	xi
Introduction	1
1 How it all began	7
2 Rationale for change	29
3 Enabling environments	41
4 Putting ideas into practice	53
5 Barriers to implementation	83
6 Transitions	97
7 Moving forward – Year 1 and beyond	113
Afterword	121
Index	123

List of figures

1.1	Child A EYFS profile results	20
1.2	Child B EYFS profile results	20
1.3	Year 1 Timetable September	22
1.4	Year 1 Timetable October onwards	24
1.5	Practical maths activity	25
1.6	Maths worksheet	25
1.7	Writing for pleasure	26
1.8	Girl writing outdoors	27
3.1	Planning the classroom environment around a core text	42
3.2	Planning the classroom environment around a core text	42
3.3	Planning the classroom environment around a core text	43
3.4	Planning the classroom environment around a core text	43
3.5	Rainforest investigation area	44
3.6	Owl Babies, small world play and writing opportunities	45
3.7	Chinese New Year	45
3.8	Role play café	46
3.9	Three boys working together	47
3.10	Maths outdoors	48
3.11	Maths outdoors	49
4.1	Characteristics of effective learning	54
4.2	Creative workshop shared area	65
4.3	Storing resources shared area	65
4.4	Medium-term plan: *The Three Little Pigs*	68
4.5	Boy's writing – September	69
4.6	Boy's writing – March	69
4.7	Science investigation area	74
4.8	Science investigation area	75
4.9	Science investigation area	75
4.10	Science investigation area	76
4.11	Medium-term plan: Superheroes	77

4.12	Medium-term plan: Pirates	78
5.1	Girl's writing – September	88
5.2	Improvement in writing skills over six months	88
5.3	Small world prompt sheet	91
5.4	Practical maths activity	94
6.1	What I have enjoyed most at school this year	102
6.2	What I have enjoyed most at school this year	103
6.3	Transition action plan	105
6.4	Blank transition action plan	106
6.5	Leaflet for parents – play-based learning	107
6.6	Leaflet for parents – planning around a core text	108

Preface

Let Me Be 5

Let me be 5 …

I like to make mess and take risks,

I like the great outdoors,

I am an active learner and like to work with my friends,

I am not ready to sit at a desk all day,

I still need to play, explore and be creative.

Don't make me grow up too quickly!

Acknowledgments

This book is a result of our experiences of observing children who had been lively, motivated learners in their Reception classes, struggle to cope with the demands of a formal Year 1 approach. We saw children fidgeting whilst sitting on the carpet, finding an hour-long English and Maths lesson too long to sit at a table and missing the opportunity for play which was such a feature of their experience of the Early Years Foundation Stage; we also recognised that conscientious, committed teachers were finding it difficult to ensure children maintained concentration as they tried to deliver whole class lessons. We knew there had to be a better way to manage the transition from a play-based to a subject-based curriculum and that expecting our five-year-old children to settle down to formal whole-class lessons as soon as they moved into Year 1 was not right. Our work to provide a manageable balance between the demands of the Key Stage 1 subject-based curriculum and the developmental needs of our young children could not have happened without the support of the staff and children across the Swale Academies Trust and the staff and children of other schools with whom we have been privileged to work.

Our thanks go to Mike Wilson, *Director of Primaries*, Swale Academies Trust, whose determination that we must provide all children, and especially the disadvantaged, with experiences that will promote curiosity, active learning, co-operation and engagement and so foster a love of learning, typifies his principled approach to leadership. His support, along with his constant encouragement, has enabled us to help staff transform Year 1 provision for so many children. Our thanks go as well to the staff and children of Istead Rise Primary School in Kent and, in particular, to Mathew Currie, head of school and to Karen Underdown, whose enthusiasm and energy have provided the children in her classes with confidence in themselves, fun and some memorable experiences. We are also indebted to the Year 1 staff at Westlands Primary School who willingly agreed to trial our ideas and who gave us valuable feedback. We are grateful to Jo Wood from Beaver Green Primary School in Ashford, Kent, who eloquently describes how she disseminated the knowledge she had gained at Westlands Primary School to other schools in the Trust. Thanks are also due to Michelle Aldred, executive headteacher at James Dixon Primary School and to Fred Banks, assistant headteacher, who has helped us with much of the material for Chapter 7. Fred's passionate belief that all children, regardless of age, should continue to enjoy experiential, active learning and engage with the outdoors, has benefited a huge number of children who have been fortunate to pass through the school.

We are also indebted to schools beyond the Swale Academies Trust who have welcomed us and provided a wealth of information and ideas. Thanks go to Louise Robertson, headteacher of Allen Edwards School in Stockwell, London, and a member of her staff who explained so honestly the challenges she faced – and overcame – in her first few weeks in Year 1 and who was so appreciative of the support of staff from the Early Years Foundation Stage. We are also grateful to Anna Jackson, headteacher of Peel Clothworkers School in the Isle of Man, where the Year 1 classroom was set up to be challenging, creative and an exciting place to be. Liz Laws, headteacher of Pickhurst Infant Academy in Bromley, South London, and her deputy, Lee Pender, showed us how teachers can provide a rich, stimulating curriculum in which children were deeply immersed and engaged in their learning, even though both physical and human resources were limited, compared to many schools. At Rockmount Primary School in Croydon, South London, a seamless transition from Nursery to Reception through to Year 1 has been embedded for many years and the three year groups operate as a single phase in the school. The learning environment provides a wealth of opportunity for children to become engrossed and absorbed and we are grateful to Tracey Langridge and Helen Carvall, the two co-heads, along with Amber Pearless, assistant headteacher and the EYFS and Year 1 lead, who have allowed us to use photographs of some of the thought-provoking and imaginative activities they provide.

Introduction

It is the end of October. In a Year 1 class in a small primary school in north-west Kent, a group of children are desperately trying to help Batwoman free their favourite super-heroes. In order to do this, they have to find the right key to unlock a padlock. The only way they can free each superhero is by solving an addition or subtraction problem using numbers to 20.

Lucy carefully works out the answer to her calculation and having used a number line to calculate that $13 - 5 = 8$, delightedly exclaims "Its 8 – I freed him with number 8!" Elsewhere in the classroom, children shine torches on to paper bats hanging from the ceiling so they can read the calculations written there – they use a range of resources, including number lines and counters, to work out the answers, sometimes working alone, sometimes deciding to work with others, but always absorbed in their tasks.

Outside, a five-year-old boy concentrates for over 15 minutes as he writes about the evil pea that escaped from the freezer in his retelling of the story of "Supertato" (Hendra and Linnet 2014); the book the class are reading. The classroom and outdoor learning area are vibrant and reflect the book the children are reading as well as their interest in ghosts, spiders and bats (it is Hallowe'en!). Outside, children are using small world props to retell the story of "Supertato"; they are shooting water pistols at words which they then use in a sentence and designing their own superheroes made from real vegetables. Both indoors and outside, all children are engrossed in their tasks, collaborating happily and fully engaged. One adult works with a small group whilst the other moves round the indoor and outdoor learning areas, encouraging any children who need help and facilitating their learning through sensitive, relaxed intervention.

Two years earlier, in another school, a class of Year 1 children were sitting at tables, laboriously trying to write a story opening. The classroom was very similar to a Year 4 room – there were tables and chairs set out in groups, lists of words on the walls and vocabulary mats on the tables. There was a small book corner but few other resources. The teacher was walking round the class encouraging the pupils to write. He had a warm, friendly manner but there is little doubt he was struggling to keep all pupils on task and he was definitely working harder than the children! After 40 minutes, a few children (mainly girls) had written three or four sentences, all of which started "Once upon a time …" However, the majority of children were fidgety, bored and reluctant to write.

It was this type of provision, sadly still very common in Year 1 classes, which inspired us to look at what we are expecting of our Year 1 children – and their teachers. This latter experience was almost universally replicated over each of our schools as they joined our Trust. We firmly believe that children in Year 1 should continue to experience a child-centred, play-based curriculum that builds on their prior attainment. The principles underpinning the Early Years Foundation Stage (EYFS) are equally relevant to older children. In order to continue to develop resilience, independence and reflection, the *Characteristics of Effective Learning*, a fundamental basis of the approach to learning and development set out in the *Statutory Framework for the Early Years Foundation Stage* (2018), must underpin learning across Year 1 and beyond. As McDowall Clark, talking about children's experiences in Reception, states: "Despite good intentions on all sides, the power of external expectations can result in attempts to fit young children into the requirements of school and the curriculum rather than the other way round" (McDowall Clark 2017, p. 100).

Senior leaders, in particular, may have little direct experience of teaching younger children. Mindful of performance tables including EYFS profile results, the end of Year 1 phonics screening check, the end of KS1 SATs and beyond, they often see a didactic approach to teaching as being the most effective in securing results. Research (Phillips and Stipek 1993) indicates there may be some evidence of short-term gains; however, didactic approaches appear to undermine young children's motivation in, and enjoyment of, school and often have negative implications for long-term achievement,

This book sets out to demonstrate that adapting what is taught to children's interests and developmental needs does not at all conflict with high standards of attainment; in fact, our experience shows the reverse is true.

Our approach has been different from that of some other practitioners who have advocated maintaining a completely play-based, child-led approach in Year 1. Whilst recognising this can be very successful in schools where staff fully understand and are committed to that philosophy, this book is aimed at those schools where teachers and senior leaders recognise that transition from Reception to Year 1 is a problem for many of their children and staff, but who do not know how to go about finding a middle ground between what is often perceived as a lack of structure in EYFS and the demands of a subject-based curriculum. Our approach may not suit everyone and we are constantly adapting and changing our practice as teachers become more confident in letting children lead the learning. What we are advocating is a playful approach to learning, building on what children know and can do. In our Year 1 classrooms there is a mixture of child-initiated and adult-initiated play-based activities along with some short whole-class, though more often small group, adult-directed sessions. How we do this is set out in Chapters 3 and 4.

Terminology

In the book the use of the term "teacher" means any adult supporting children's learning in the classroom. This could include teaching assistants or learning support assistants, as well as class teachers. Children are referred to randomly as "he" or "she." Pseudonyms have been used when referring to individual children.

The authors

The co-authors of this book are both senior leaders in the Swale Academies Trust, a multi-academy trust made up of ten primary schools in London, Kent and East Sussex, a nursery in Kent and five secondary schools in Kent and East Sussex. Victoria Pettett is now head of school of Westlands Primary School, a large three-form entry primary school in Sittingbourne, Kent. She has been the EYFS lead at the school for a number of years and is also the lead Early Years practitioner for the Trust. Sue Quirk has worked as an advisory headteacher for the Trust for a number of years, having been a headteacher and a school improvement adviser in two local authorities in London. She also worked as a school improvement partner, a school improvement advisor assessor and as an independent consultant. She is also chair of governors at a primary school in Central London. Although many examples in the book are drawn from schools within the Swale Academies Trust we have also been fortunate to work with a number of other schools, in particular, Allen Edwards Primary School, an inner-city school in Lambeth, Rockmount Primary School in outer London, Peel Clothworkers School in the Isle of Man and Pickhurst Infant Academy in Bromley, south-east London.

Structure of the book

Chapter 1 describes the journey made by staff and children as they joined the Swale Academies Trust and focuses on the reasons senior leaders made a commitment to investing in the Early Years and how they went about it.

In Chapter 2 the authors describe how, in their role as senior leaders within a multi-academy trust, they observed Year 1 teachers working really hard teaching writing or Mathematics to a whole class. Children were passively sitting at tables, working individually, often filling in worksheets and many were struggling to record their work. The authors recognised these were the same children who just a few weeks earlier had been independent, enthusiastic learners sharing their ideas with their peers. A number of children, especially boys, were being identified as having behavioural problems because they were not developmentally ready to sit at tables and chairs for long periods. One of the authors reflects on the challenges she faced when teaching a Year 1 class early in her career. The impact of the confusion between curriculum and pedagogy on children's well-being and mental health are considered.

Chapters 3 and 4 describe how we put our ideas into practice. Chapter 3 concentrates on developing a classroom environment that promotes play-based learning whilst Chapter 4 explores ways of addressing the subject-based curriculum of Key Stage 1 and sets out what this could look like at different times of the day. The authors discuss how children in Year 1 should continue to experience a child–centred curriculum that builds on their prior attainment because the principles underpinning the EYFS curriculum, are equally relevant to older children. They stress the importance of this approach for disadvantaged children. They explore how children in Year 1 should continue to develop the independence that characterises good EYFS practice with the use of a well–resourced indoor and outdoor environment. Teaching in Year 1 is often more effective when it is closely targeted and focused at small groups within enabling environments. In addition, the authors argue that, in order to continue to develop resilience, independence and reflection, the *Characteristics of Effective Learning*, which typify effective practice in the EYFS curriculum, should continue to underpin learning across Year 1. There are examples of how the authors worked with various schools within the Swale Academies Trust to change provision in Year 1, with samples of timetables and photographs of effective classroom set-up and activities. It includes photographs of different ways teachers "think outside of the box" when planning activities so children are not sitting passively or filling in worksheets.

In Chapter 5, the authors consider barriers to adopting a play-based pedagogy in Year 1. These include external pressures, such as the need for schools to perform well in assessments like the Year 1 phonics screening check and the KS1 SATs assessments in Year 2. Many school leaders are anxious to ensure pupils are "ready" for these assessments and feel pressurised into adopting a more formal approach to learning. Some school leaders have voiced concerns about perceptions that they will be adversely judged by Ofsted – and the authors discuss how Ofsted's publication *Bold Beginnings* (Ofsted 2017) may have strengthened these perceptions. The chapter also considers parental expectations and issues of resourcing and managing time in a subject-based curriculum. It explores the uncertainty faced by Year 1 teachers on how best to deliver the Year 1 curriculum to ensure that by the end of the year, children are able to meet the more demanding requirements of the new curriculum and are well prepared to enter Year 2.

Chapter 6 explores transitions from EYFS to Year 1, Year 1 to Year 2 and Year 2 and beyond. In order to support continuity of learning from EYFS into Year 1, the authors consider the need for a carefully planned transition. This includes Reception staff spending time with their Year 1 colleagues explaining the judgments which led to the end of EYFS assessments especially in writing and Mathematics. The authors discuss how Year 1 teachers should understand the difference between a child who has been assessed as expected or exceeding and know the next steps for those children. Year 1 teachers should also know that children who did not achieve a Good Level of Development might have met the expected standards in reading, writing and Mathematics. The authors consider how Reception teachers could support Year 1 colleagues with the first week's planning as they know the children, their interests and abilities. They also look at views from parents of children who have moved from EYFS to Year 1 as part of their action research and the need to continue to plan for positive enrichment activities. Chapter 6 also looks at the importance of involving parents in their child's education. When children start school, parents are invited in to meet their child's new teacher, they are encouraged to come into the classroom and their children's work is shared with them regularly. Parents are used to regular, often daily contact with the school when children are in EYFS, so why does this have to stop? The authors recognise that transition can be hard for parents as well as children and in order for transitions to be successful, there should be a shared approach from everybody involved.

In the final chapter, the authors consider how they might develop their work across older year groups. They consider how the principles and benefits of continuing to adopt specific elements of a play-based curriculum could work as children move further up the school. They draw on the work being developed at one of the schools in the Swale Academies Trust. They discuss how creating a context for learning, linking activities to a core text, continuing to make use of outdoor learning and focussing on enabling environments continue to be relevant for children in Key Stage 2 and beyond.

How should the book be used and what will readers gain?

The book sets out to show that there is no reason why children who are just five years old, should have to change the way they learn, simply because they are starting in Year 1. There is something in this book for everyone involved with children of this age. Chapter 1 explains the reasons we made a leap of faith into changing the practice of decades and Chapter 2 sets out the research which underpins our arguments. Chapter 2, in particular, will be of interest to students, school leaders and academics. Chapters 3 and 4 give practical advice on how to set up the learning environments and implement timetables and lesson plans which will be of particular relevance to teachers, teaching assistants and anyone working in schools. School leaders and governors will find Chapter 5 – which considers the barriers to implementing a play-based approach for five-year-old children – helpful in addressing concerns over standards and external pressures. Parents and children, as well as teachers, will recognise the issues over transition explored in Chapter 6. Students training to be primary school teachers and parents, as well as those working at all levels in schools, are likely to find Chapter 7 of particular interest as it describes how children up to Year 6 in primary schools can benefit from a curriculum based on the principles of play-based learning.

More than anything else, our hope is that this book will give all those involved with young children's learning, the confidence to resist the pressure to adopt a formal approach to learning too early and to let our children enjoy being five years old!

References

Department for Education (2018) *Statutory Framework for the Early Years Foundation Stage*. Available at https://www.gov.uk/government/publications/early-years-foundation-stage-framework--2 (Accessed 11 March 2019).

Hendra, S. and Linnet, P. (2014) *Supertato*. London: Simon & Schuster.

McDowall Clark, R. (2017) *Exploring the Contexts for Early Learning*. Oxford: Routledge.

Ofsted (2017) *Bold Beginnings: The Reception Curriculum in a Sample of Good and Outstanding Primary Schools*, November 2017, No. 170045. Manchester: Ofsted.

Phillips, D. and Stipek, D. (1993) Early Formal Schooling: Are We Promoting Achievement or Anxiety? *Applied and Preventive Psychology: Current Scientific Directions* 2 (3), 141–150.

How it all began

The Swale Academies Trust, based in Kent, came into being in September 2010 as one of the first Academy Converter Schools centred around Westlands Secondary School in Sittingbourne. Westlands Primary School, one of the main feeder primary schools for Westlands Secondary School, was the first primary school to join the Trust, followed soon after by Regis Manor Primary School in Milton Regis, just outside Sittingbourne.

For a number of years, Westlands Primary School had struggled with low academic standards and high staff turnover. On more than one occasion, the school had failed to meet the government floor standards, which set the minimum expectations for pupils' attainment and progress by the end of Key Stage 2 and soon after joining the Trust, the school was judged by Ofsted to have Serious Weaknesses.

Fortunately, by this time the Trust had put into place a number of measures to tackle the legacy of underachievement, including the appointment of a primary lead who became executive headteacher and who had a wealth of experience in working with schools in difficulties. He had an excellent track record of working with existing teams of teachers and support staff, recognising individual strengths and building strong teams who understood how young children learn. Crucially, he was adamant that conditions for learning needed to be right for the very youngest children.

In an interview, he commented:

Many failing schools are those in challenging circumstances with a high proportion of disadvantaged children. With the youngest children we have one opportunity to get it right in developing positive attitudes to future learning – it's much harder to turn it round later.

A play-based curriculum based on children's interests will appeal to a diverse set of needs. It has to start with planning experiences that will promote curiosity, active learning, co-operation and engagement and so foster a love of learning – if these are not in place by the time a child has finished the Early Years Foundation Stage, there will be huge gaps which are difficult to fill later. Good Early Years provision gives a level playing field where all children can access learning experiences which appeal to them.

However, high-quality Early Years provision needs investment — not just of excellent resources, indoors and outside, but also people. Poor subject knowledge at any stage is a barrier to children thriving. It's important to put strong teachers and teaching assistants in Reception and to continue to provide high-quality continuing professional development for all adults, so all early years practitioners have a deep understanding of pedagogy and how children grow and develop.

(Mike Wilson, interview, 2020)

Getting it right for the youngest children

As the Trust grew and took on more schools, almost all facing significant challenges and difficulties (there are currently ten primary schools in the Trust, in Kent, south-east London and East Sussex) a key priority was to invest time, staff professional development and resources into the Early Years Foundation Stage (EYFS). Over the next two or three years, capacity at senior leadership level within the Trust was enhanced. A Primary Improvement team was formed consisting of the primary lead (by now the Director of Primaries) and two advisory headteachers, one of whom is one of the authors of this book. They were responsible for ensuring that all the primary schools in the Trust were successful, effective schools with high standards of achievement where all children would benefit from a high-quality education where they would be seen as special, unique and exceptionally well cared for.

This book is by no means a plug for academies. We recognise many local authorities have the highest standards in holding schools to account and supporting and challenging them. One of the authors has recently worked as a school improvement adviser in a high-performing inner London local authority, where the vast majority of primary schools have opted to remain within local authority control. However, regardless of the type of school, it is self-evident that effective leadership which promotes capacity building, collaboration and continuing professional development (CPD) is the key to ensuring children thrive and make the progress of which they are capable. The Swale Academies Trust's approach to working with their schools is set out on its website:

Where we differ from many Trusts is that we seek to help support individual schools to grow and develop their own good practice. A key feature of our work is the mentoring and development of leadership teams to enable them to focus and act upon things effectively and at the right time. We develop existing teams of teachers and support staff through high-quality professional development. It is noticeable that in all of the schools we have developed, the majority of the staff who were present when the school fell into crisis are still there at the point when the school emerges from its difficulties. This only occurs when the organisation values the individual and recognises that competence is often relative to the level of high-quality professional development received and acted upon.

(Swale Academies Trust website, 2019)

The Early Years lead at Westlands Primary School at the time (now Head of School, Early Years Lead across the Trust and the other co-author of this book) recognised that the school's approach to the learning and development of children in the EYFS was not meeting the needs of the children in her care. She knew that the formal subject-based methodology, which historically had been the school's preferred approach, was inappropriate. She already had a clear understanding of effective Early Years' pedagogy – her degree was in early childhood studies – but the school, in line with many others at that time, implemented a more formal approach to the EYFS curriculum.

The Director of Primaries for the Trust arranged for her to spend two days at a school in another local authority where he had previously been the headteacher, which had an outstanding EYFS department. By spending two full days working as part of the EYFS team at Rockmount Primary School in Croydon, Victoria was able to immerse herself fully in the planning, observation and assessment cycle. She saw how staff planned activities based around children's interests, how the learning environments, both inside and outdoors, were set up to provide stimulating challenges which enabled children to make rapid progress in their learning and development and how adults sensitively engaged and interacted with children to promote warm, positive relationships within a culture of high expectations for all. Working as part of the team, she joined in with staff setting up the activities for the day, taking part in discussions at the end of the day about individual children's achievements and planning their next steps. On her return to Westlands Primary School, Victoria's enthusiasm for change was contagious and her confidence inspired other members of her team to follow her lead. Knowing she was well supported by the senior leadership of the Trust, and having seen how effective the provision at Rockmount was, within a very short space of time, the learning environment had been transformed, short-term, flexible planning was centred around children's interests and a play-based curriculum was in place.

Disseminating effective practice

The next few years were a busy time as other schools from Kent, south-east London and further afield joined the Trust. The approach of immersing staff in a successful EYFS setting has been replicated as other schools have joined the Trust – although now there is sufficient capacity within the Trust for staff not to have to travel to other schools. Senior leaders within the Trust recognised the impact of the strategy and agreed to release some staff for a full week as part of their professional development. It would be disingenuous to claim that all staff have taken on board the learning from this experience as quickly and as comprehensively as was the case with Westlands Primary School. Each school is different; the capacity of individual members of staff to take on the pace of change is never the same; people relocate, go on maternity or paternity leave and need different degrees of support at different times. However, the approach of working as a member of the team in an effective Early Years' provision where staff know children really well, plan activities around children's interests and are skilled in supporting and extending children's play has proved to be a highly effective strategy in helping staff to understand the rationale and principles underlying effective teaching and learning in an early years' setting.

At the time of writing, there are ten primary schools in the Trust and each has a strong, child-centred, play-based Early Years provision. The EYFS lead at Beaver Green Primary School in Ashford in Kent was one of the teachers at Westlands Primary School and worked closely with Victoria, so was able to disseminate the way we worked. When asking about her experience, she said:

When I arrived at Beaver Green Primary School, the setting was very formal. The majority of the day in the Reception classes was spent as teacher-directed time, where ALL of the children were expected to sit down and write in an exercise book every day. I was given the role of EYFS lead and with the support of the Senior Leadership Team within the Trust was able to change the provision to mirror the approach which was in place at Westlands Primary School. Letting children lead the learning and going with their interests gets the children excited about learning and leads to excellent progress. Writing is still happening on a daily basis in our free flow approach, but the children are writing about what interests them, in a way that they feel comfortable. This may be on clipboards outside, chalks, they may be lying on the floor with large paper, or writing on paper stuck under a table.

From working at Westlands Primary School, I had learned the importance of linking the provision to a core text. Finding out what the children's interests were through home visits, and speaking to Nurseries, we would then have an overarching topic for a short term. A high-quality core text (linked to this topic) formed the basis of the learning, which would engage and enthuse children. All areas of learning would be linked to this core text throughout free flow.

One of the most important things I learned, was the critical role of adults in facilitating children's learning. Specific training was required for all staff to develop their understanding of the importance of asking open-ended questions and to extend the quality of play. Adults can scaffold and extend children's play, by encouraging children to add resources and props and by posing exciting challenges. The adult also needs to be aware of the individual needs of the children and their next steps and how best to support these within the provision.

We gathered evidence of achievements during free flow time, which happened during the majority of the day. Teacher-directed time is very limited as we recognised that children demonstrate their highest level of skills, knowledge and understanding when they are absorbed in their play. It is the teacher's job to ensure that activities interest the children and they are planning for each area of development, for example making sure writing opportunities are available everywhere – especially outside. Even the most resistant writers will be grabbing a pen when it is something in which they are interested and excited! Moving into Year 1 it is important to continue this approach.

(Jo Wood, interview, 2019)

Developing play-based learning in Year 1

Having reached the point in the development of the Trust where the EYFS provision in each of the schools was of a consistently high standard, we recognised we needed to rethink our approach to transition into Year 1. It was decided to trial a play-based approach to the curriculum at Westlands Primary School and this work was led by Victoria, who by now was an assistant headteacher at the school. Staff spent time looking at the National Curriculum end of year objectives for Year 1 and planning how these could be covered in the context of a play-based approach. A key priority at the time was to develop children's writing skills; opportunities for mark making and writing were everywhere in our EYFS settings; clipboards by the construction area, whiteboards and marker pens by the bikes to record whose turn it was, large sheets of paper rolled out on the floor, along with blank booklets and leaflets by tabletop displays. One of the many challenges was how to replicate those opportunities in Year 1 classrooms which traditionally had chairs and tables for 30 children. Under Victoria's guidance, staff developed a framework which included discrete times for teaching the core subjects of English and Mathematics, but also provided a classroom environment which allowed children to access a range of independent learning activities (continuous provision) including opportunities for children to write for a range of purposes, as well as to explore cross-curricular learning. This involved removing most of the furniture, leaving just enough tables and chairs for up to 12 children to be seated at a table at any one time. This then freed up space for construction, small world play, creative experiences, exploration and investigation.

During the course of the year, staff trialled and refined their approach. One of the biggest challenges for teachers, especially those who had little experience of teaching the very youngest children, was to see themselves not as instructors and imparters of knowledge but as facilitators and scaffolders of learning. For many teachers, who had been used to planning to meet the requirements of a National Curriculum objective by delivering a whole-class input on the carpet, followed by differentiated activities, this was a major paradigm shift. Once again, the importance of strong leadership was key and teachers were supported with help in setting up the environment, by being given time to plan and reflect on children's responses and by working alongside senior leaders who modelled how to use the environment to promote a play-based approach to cross-curricular learning.

The Director of Primaries was highly supportive of this change of approach to teaching in Year 1. He commented:

Children develop at different stages and not all children are ready for formal learning on 1st September in Year 1. It is important to understand what has been effective about the play-based approach in EYFS and it makes sense to continue to maintain this way of working as children move into Key Stage 1. Year 1 teachers have a wealth of knowledge about children's achievements because the EYFS profile gives more information across a whole range of domains, including their Personal, Social, Emotional and Physical Development, than at any other stage of a child's education. When transition to a more formal way of working takes place too early, there will be missed opportunities to see what children can do.

(Mike Wilson, 2020)

He also stressed the importance of leaders being able to understand and articulate the learning that is taking place in a child-initiated, play-based environment.

Some teachers and support staff took on this new approach quickly whilst others took much longer to adjust. By referring constantly to the principles underpinning the EYFS curriculum, and showing how they are equally relevant to older children and by referring to the Characteristics of Effective Learning, which form the basis of the Early Years framework and again are relevant to learners of all ages, leaders were able to support staff in gradually developing a shared understanding of what teaching and learning in Year 1 could look like.

The Characteristics of Effective Learning were developed as part of the *Early Years Foundation Stage Statutory Framework* (Department for Education, 2018). That document states:

> *In planning and guiding children's activities, practitioners must reflect on the different ways that children learn and reflect these in their practice. Three characteristics of effective teaching and learning are:*
>
> ***Playing and exploring** – Children investigate and experience things, and "have a go."*
>
> ***Active learning** – Children concentrate and keep on trying if they encounter difficulties, and enjoy achievements.*
>
> ***Creating and thinking critically** – Children have and develop their own ideas, make links between ideas, and develop strategies for doing things.*

Although the Year 1 staff at Westlands Primary School would be the first to admit they were still on a journey, by now there was a framework in place in which children were engaged and clearly making progress and which was sufficiently flexible for other schools within the Trust to trial. Chapter 4 covers in detail what the provision looks like at different times during the day and how we developed our approaches to teaching and learning in Year 1.

Developing a consistent approach across all the schools

During the summer term, the co-authors of this book visited every school in the Trust to look at provision in Year 1. We discussed our findings with staff, headteachers and with the Primary Improvement team and knew we had their agreement and support to change the way our Year 1 classes were working. In July of that year, we brought together all the Year 1 teachers and Early Years leads for a day's training on how to prepare for the coming academic year. We made the day practical, looking at principles, the rationale for change, transition at various points, enabling environments, timetables, planning and assessment. The sessions were interspersed with visits to the three Year 1 classrooms at different times of the day. We arranged for staff to talk to the Year 1 teachers about their experiences and encouraged them to be honest about the barriers and difficulties as well as the successes. We produced a guidance document which set out the learning that had taken place and which staff could use as they implemented, what to many was, a completely new way of working. A copy of this document is to be found at the end of this chapter (Appendix 1) and is available for schools to use as they wish.

During the following year, the two co-authors continued to support staff through visits to schools, arranging meetings for Year 1 staff to share ideas, celebrate successes and problem solve and by disseminating good practice, such as that described in the Introduction. Throughout the year, we visited all the Year 1 classes and worked with teachers and teaching assistants to support them in the change to their practice, notably in the move away from whole-class teaching and in continuing to provide opportunities for children to continue to learn in the ways they had done whilst in Reception.

A number of practical issues arose during the year. These included:

- We had to challenge the perception that every child needed to be able to sit at a table at the same time. It is difficult to deliver a play-based curriculum in most average-sized classrooms if tables and chairs for up to 30 children are in place. As discussed above, if tables and chairs are available for up to 12 children to work with an adult or in a focussed group at any one time, this gives teachers flexibility to adapt the way they organise the classroom and to provide activities such as a writing table, small world activities, construction, investigative and creative activities. If storage of furniture is a problem, there is no reason why some of these activities cannot be set out on tables, but we do not expect every child to be sitting at a table, formally recording work. Some examples of how we set out our classrooms are found in Chapter 3.

- Staff found they were spending a significant period of time at lunchtime in setting up the classroom for the afternoon sessions. This gradually became less of an issue during the year as staff became adept at quickly putting out other activities that had been prepared that morning and adapting and extending some of the activities that had been provided during the morning.

- In some schools, staff needed reassurance that not everything had to be formally recorded for "evidence." Tracking systems, as described in Chapter 4, helped to ensure coverage of foundation subjects.

- Staffing ratios might need to be reviewed, especially towards the beginning of the year. For example, in a two-form entry school each class will need a full-time teacher, and ideally a full-time teaching assistant. However, we recognise this is not always possible and, as described in Chapter 5, many schools manage with fewer staff than this.

- We were fortunate in that in all our schools our Year 1 classrooms had access to an outdoor learning area, although this was not always directly accessible from the classroom. We recognise this may not be the case in all schools.

- Schools need to be flexible and acutely responsive to the needs of children. For some cohorts, it may be necessary to continue with EYFS provision for a longer period in Term 1.

- Schools should also consider how they will maintain a strong partnership with parents. In some schools, it may be possible to invite parents in for part of the day to share their children's learning.

Successes and challenges

We met with the Year 1 teachers in March of that year to review what had gone well, what needed to be addressed and to plan for transition to Year 2.

Aspects that had gone well included:

- Teachers recognised the importance of continuing to promote spiritual, moral, social and cultural development through a range of enrichment activities. Memorable occasions that enable children to experience awe and wonder and a fascination with the world enhance their learning across a wide range of curriculum subjects.

- Senior leaders in schools had supported their staff well and provided reassurance.

- Relationships were warm and positive – staff were encouraging and nurturing. Staff were broadly positive about the changes – the biggest challenge for some teachers was allowing children to lead the learning! It was a real culture shock for some teachers to realise that children following their interests during free flow activities were often far more deeply engaged in cross-curricular learning than they would ever have been in a carpet session led by the teacher.

- Pupils demonstrated high levels of engagement during small group activities and during free flow. They worked collaboratively, helping each other, and almost all children were engaged almost all of the time in purposeful, practical activities.

- By working with small mixed-ability groups in writing, children made rapid progress and teachers were able to provide targeted support and instant feedback.

- Small, focussed teaching groups in Mathematics meant that teachers were able to assess children's understanding accurately and address misconceptions immediately. Well-planned Maths activities in the continuous provision meant that children were able to consolidate and apply their learning.

- Classroom environments were well organised, with a range of cross-curricular activities both indoors and out and displays which supported and celebrated children's learning.

- With the pressure of whole-class teaching removed, once teachers had familiarised themselves with the approach to learning, they were more relaxed, and able to get to know their children really well.

Areas which needed further work included:

- All schools could benefit from reviewing how they challenge the most able pupils. Whilst work was often well pitched during focussed small group work, there were often missed opportunities during short whole-class carpet sessions to set the most able children independent challenges or problem-solving activities.

- We also need to consider how to ensure that all independent learning activities are open ended enough to allow children to challenge themselves during free flow sessions – as Bryce Clegg (2017) pointed out, high levels of engagement do not necessarily mean high levels of attainment. Chapters 3 and 4 give examples of a number of open-ended activities which encourage children to explore further and deeper.

Two years later, as the Trust is still growing, most of our schools have taken on a play-based learning approach to Year 1 and teachers recognise children's levels of engagement, enthusiasm for learning and independence. They are confident that children are benefiting from meaningful learning experiences. As one teacher said: *"There's no way I would go back to how we used to do it !"*

Summary

Children develop at different rates and not all are ready for a formal way of working at the start of Year 1. However, implementing and managing change takes time and thought. Developing a play-based approach to a subject-based curriculum requires skill and insight and is likely to require a significant investment in resources, including staff training. It is important that all staff, especially those in senior positions in a school, understand how children in the EYFS can make rapid progress in their skills, knowledge and understanding over a range of domains and how this way of working can be transferred to Year 1 and beyond.

> **REFLECTION**
>
> ■ How far do you agree with the philosophy that in order to build a successful school, it is essential to start by ensuring there is high-quality provision for the youngest children?
>
> ■ How much should Year 1 classrooms mirror the provision in EYFS?
>
> ■ How easy would it be in your school to challenge the perceptions of what teaching in Year 1 should look like?

References

Bryce Clegg, A. (2017) *Effective Transition into Year 1*. London: Featherstone Education.

Department for Education (2018) *Statutory Framework for the Early Years Foundation Stage*. Available at: https://www.gov.uk/government/publications/early-years-foundation-stage-framework--2 (Accessed: 11 March 2019).

Swale Academies Trust website (2019) Available at: https://www.swale.at (Accessed 22 October 2019).

Appendix 1
Year 1 provision

A shared understanding

A one-day training programme for EYFS and Year 1 staff across the Swale Academies Trust

Aims of the day

By the end of today we will have a shared understanding of effective provision for Year 1 children across the Trust.

We will look at:

- Rationale
- Principles
- Transition
- Enabling environments
- Timetables
- Planning formats
- Year 1 practice at Westlands Primary School

Rationale

The transition from Foundation Stage to Key Stage 1 remains an area for development in schools across the country. Some of the issues include:

- Ineffective use of assessment.
- Lack of continuity and progression in provision for learning in Year 1.
- Lack of understanding of the importance of a practical, play-based approach to learning.
- Children start Year 1 having experienced a play-based curriculum in EYFS where they have been encouraged to develop independence by making their own choices about resources, activities and whether these take place indoors or outside.
- Teaching in Year 1 can bring its own set of unique challenges; in many schools, teachers are uncertain how to best deliver the Year 1 curriculum to ensure that by the end of the year, children are able to meet the more demanding requirements of the new curriculum and are well prepared to enter Year 2. Many schools feel that time for play is over when children start Year 1 and that it is important to get children ready for Year 2 and beyond. This is not the approach we take.
- During Year 1, children develop their core strength and become developmentally more ready to acquire the stamina they will need to concentrate and sustain attention for longer periods.
- Today we are going to look at ways to support teachers to plan appropriate provision to meet the needs of 5- and 6-year-olds.

Principles into practice

The principles underpinning the EYFS curriculum, listed here, are equally relevant to older children:

- Every child is a unique child, who is constantly learning and can be resilient, capable, confident and self-assured.
- Children learn to be strong and independent through positive relationships.
- Children learn and develop well in enabling environments, in which their experiences respond to their individual needs and there is a strong partnership between practitioners and parents or carers.
- Children develop and learn in different ways and at different rates.

- In Year 1 children should be given the opportunity to build upon and develop the independence that characterises good EYFS practice.

- Opportunities are needed for children both indoors and outdoors.

- A balance between child-initiated and adult-directed activities.

- Planning should take into account the interests of the children.

Characteristics of effective learning

The Characteristics of Effective Learning underpin all areas of development and should move through all subjects further up the school. These include:

Playing and exploring – *Children investigate and experience things, and "have a go".*

Active learning – *Children concentrate and keep on trying if they encounter difficulties, and enjoy achievements.*

Creating and thinking critically – *Children have and develop their own ideas, make links between ideas, and develop strategies for doing things.*

Activity – *Discuss the extent to which you think these principles and Characteristics of Effective Learning can be applied to a subject-based curriculum.*

A good level of development

Teaching and Learning in Year 1 needs to be child-centred to meet the needs of children who did not achieve a good level of development (GLD) at the end of the Early Years Foundation Stage (EYFS). These children should be reassessed at the end of Term 1 and if necessary, at the end of Term 2. Children who are still not meeting that standard may need a referral to the schools SENDCo.

A child is assessed as having a "good level of development" if they met the criteria for "expected" or "exceeding" in the first 12 early learning goals. These are:

Communication and language: Listening and Attention, Understanding, Speaking

Physical development: Moving and Handling, Health and Self-care

Personal development: Self-confidence and Self-awareness, Managing Feelings and Behaviour, Making Relationships

Literacy: Reading, Writing

Child A	CL	CL	CL	PHY	PHY	PSE	PSE	PSE	LR	LW	MN	MSSM	UTW	UTW	UTW	EAD	EAD	GLD
July	2	1	1	2	2	2	2	2	1	1	1	1	2	2	2	2	2	N
Oct	2	2	2	2	2	2	2	2	1	1	2	2	2	2	2	2	2	N
Dec	2	2	2	2	2	2	2	2	2	2	2	2	2	2	2	2	2	Y

Figure 1.1 Child A EYFS profile results

Child B	CL	CL	CL	PHY	PHY	PSE	PSE	PSE	LR	LW	MN	MSSM	UTW	UTW	UTW	EAD	EAD	GLD
July	1	2	2	1	2	2	1	1	2	2	2	2	2	2	2	2	2	N
Oct	2	2	2	2	2	2	1	1	2	2	2	2	2	2	2	2	2	N
Dec	2	2	2	2	2	2	2	2	2	2	2	2	2	2	2	2	2	Y

Figure 1.2 Child B EYFS profile results

Mathematics: Number and Space, Shape and Measures

Activity: Discuss the profile judgements for Child A and Child B above, neither of whom had met the criteria for GLD by July at the end of EYFS. What sort of experiences will you need to provide to meet the needs of each child to enable them to achieve the expected standards?

Effective transition from Year R – Year 1

By late June/early July:

- Teachers to be identified for Year 1 for the next academic year.

- These teachers to be involved in moderation of work of current Year R children.

- Teachers to spend time in Reception classes (read a story at the end of the day etc.).

- TAs to spend time in the Reception classes.

- Transition meeting for parents to share approaches to learning.

- Handover meeting between Year R and Year 1 staff – data shared. Staff to discuss children's interests for Year 1 – staff to choose a topic to enthuse children in Term 1.

- Year R staff to ask children to carry out a piece of work that is about themselves (writing preferably to send to their Year 1 teacher – this is to be displayed in their new classrooms as an instant display to relate to over transition.

- Positive relationships between staff and children will be key for transition from Year R to Year 1.

"September – A new month a unique chapter"

September is a crucial month for all year groups – it is where expectations, routines and boundaries are established.

On the first day of term – staff who have been in Reception with children this year to go onto the playground around the Year 1 area ready to welcome the children back to school.

<u>Issues for teachers to think about for Term 1</u>

- Prepare the classroom environment – inside and outside – to mirror the Year 1 environment as far as possible.

- Prepare coat labels for children and self-registration cards to mirror the start of the day in Year R. Self-registration to be set up the same as in Year R.

- Have a focus on Personal, Social and Emotional Development (PSED) and the Characteristics of Effective Learning at the beginning of the term. PSED then needs to form a focus of all activities throughout the year.

- Timetable to mirror Year R for the first couple of weeks; you might like to extend the phonics session. Early morning work will be a brief session to welcome the children – the morning carpet session could include whole-class reading, shared reading and shared writing, following an audio book, reading the text from an interactive whiteboard, asking questions about the text and so on. The important thing is to keep it interactive, so children are not sitting passively. (See example timetable, Figure 1.3)

Note – 'Handwriting' is timetabled for the first session in the afternoon – this does not mean all children should be sitting at tables all copying the letter "a". Groups of children might be doing different things such as chalking letters on the playground, some children might be developing their fine motor control with activities such as using tweezers to pick up objects, threading or making patterns on small peg boards. Others will benefit from gross motor control activities, including taking part in practical sessions that involve music and movement. There are many commercial programmes available designed to improve movement and develop the particular skills needed for handwriting. In addition, other children may use whiteboards and pens to practise their letter formation.

From mid-September/early October through to Term 5

By now children should be settled into their new environments and enjoying positive relationships with the adults in their class.

It is now time to change the timetable (see page 9 – timings will vary depending on each school).

By the end of Term 1 (October), teachers should re-assess the children who did not attain a Good Level of Development at the end of Year R. to ascertain any particular areas of need. They should repeat this process in December for any children who have still not met the expected standards. For some of these children, a personalised plan might be necessary.

Suggested timetable September Year 1

	8:45 – 8:50	8:50 – 9:15	9:25 – 11.00	11:00 – 11.30	Lunchtime 11:30 – 12:45	12:45 – 1:00	1:00 – 1:25	1:20 – 2:45	2:45 – 3:15	HOMETIME 3:15
Mon.	Self registration, welcome and early work eg. Days of the week, weather, singing,	Carpet session	Free Flow	Phonics		Handwriting	Maths	Free Flow	Story Time	
Tues.		Carpet session	Free Flow	Phonics		Handwriting	Maths	Free Flow	Story Time	
Wed.		Carpet session	Free Flow	Phonics		Handwriting	Maths	Free Flow	Story Time	
Thurs.		Carpet session	Free Flow	Phonics		Handwriting	Maths	Free Flow	Story Time	
Fri.		Carpet session	Free Flow	Phonics		Handwriting	Maths	Free Flow	Story Time	

Figure 1.3 Year 1 Timetable September

Points for consideration

- We have not included assembly times, as these will vary from school to school. Staff may wish to consider the value of Year 1 children attending whole-school assemblies on a daily basis. This is something that could be introduced during the year.

- The first session in the morning will cover reading and writing skills, including phonics. This should be based around a core text and support the development of children's literacy skills through regular shared and group reading and writing interactive tasks.

- Mathematics sessions are for 45 minutes up to an hour; however, they are structured very differently from a traditional Mathematics lesson:

  - Teacher gives a short practical input with a clear learning objective (LO).

  - One adult takes a focus group carrying out an activity that is linked to the LO, the other supports the continuous provision and may well spend some time at one of the activities.

- The rest of the class are free to access the continuous provision set up around the room. In some schools, all of the independent learning activities available during this session will have a mathematical focus; in others, especially where there are no additional adults to help set up the provision before and after school, or where space is limited, some of the more open-ended continuous provision activities will be set aside or covered over, ready for the afternoon session, others will be linked to the mathematical focus, but areas such as construction and small world could remain available to children. Teachers should use their professional judgement to ensure activities are purposeful and inviting enough to engage all children. The balance of activities with a mathematical focus is likely to change through the year and will also depend on what is being taught.

Afternoon session

- At the start of the year, the afternoon session is similar to a "free flow" session in EYFS, but with teachers or teaching assistants working with groups of children for targeted group work. The afternoon starts with a whole-class carpet session at the beginning of the afternoon, when a new theme or skill is introduced. Children are then free to access the independent learning activities, with one group remaining with the teacher. This session usually focuses on the development of writing skills within a cross-curricular context, although at least once a week there is a focus on reading. We have found this to be a very effective strategy in the first two terms, with the teacher providing intensive support for children of all abilities, as it allows for instant feedback. Once children have completed their writing, they are free to access the continuous provision and the teacher will usually then take another group or perhaps support children in their free flow activities; the long uninterrupted session comfortably provides enough time for at least two groups to benefit from the teacher's focus on their writing progress.

- Whilst one group is working with the teacher, the teaching assistant will support the continuous provision and might work with other groups to address any misconceptions from the morning session or, once the children are all engaged, might lead an activity based on the theme. Many of the independent learning activities will be linked to the topic and core text and children can continue to investigate and explore the mathematical activities from the morning. Children should be able to work independently at art and design technology activities and if the outdoor learning area is available a range of activities can be set up there. There should be writing opportunities available at all activities, which children are encouraged to use.

- As the year progresses, the balance of teacher-led and child-led activities will change and towards the end of the year there may well be at least two afternoons given over to discrete subjects. The teacher-led reading and writing groups will also change with the majority of children expected to use their developing writing skills to work more independently and without the intensive adult support which was in place at the beginning of the year.

24 How it all began

Suggested timetable for Year 1 from October onwards.

	Registration/ Early morning work (up to 15 mins)	Session 1 (one hour)	Play	Session 2 (45 minutes to one hour)	Pre lunch (15 mins)	Lunch	Carpet session	Session 3 (I hour 45 minutes) (4 days a week) 5th day PE, and any subject schools wish to teach discretely.	Story time (20 mins)
Monday	Maths open ended activities – whiteboards	Literacy focus (reading, writing, phonics and grammar) based around a core text		Maths focus Whole class intro then one or two adult-led groups. Other chn practical maths activities related to learning objective, pitched to enable access for all T could teach one or two groups during this session	Whole class Phonics		Introduction to afternoon session	Two adult led groups, one with a reading or writing focus the other to address any misconceptions arising from the morning session (these could take place at different times in the afternoon so there is always an adult available to support free flow activities) Other children will take part in free flow activities linked to the topic – opportunities for writing in all activities.	
Tuesday	consolidation/ Investigation Handwriting /fine motor skills activities				Music		Topic/ theme led. Eg. Science activity Spring living creatures		
Wednesday	Interventions based on individual needs				Whole class Phonics		PE		
Thursday					PHSE/ RE whole class session		Introduction to afternoon session Topic/ theme led.		
Friday					Whole class Phonics		Eg. Science activity Spring seasonal changes		

Figure 1.4 Year 1 Timetable October onwards

Enabling environments

The environment is one part of the jigsaw to ensure support during "free flow" learning. If we get it right, children will be engaged in purposeful play of their own choice and interest.

The environment needs to:

- provide stimulation and challenge

- pick up on children's interests

- celebrate their learning

- provide resources that can be accessed independently

- encourage children's creativity and problem solving

- encourage independence and help children develop a positive attitude towards learning.

An outside area is really important to support the learning in Year 1. We do recognise that not all schools are able to do this because of the way buildings are laid out, but teachers can be creative with how they use their outside space with groups etc. It does also depend on the availability of adults, so being fully staffed is helpful. The outdoor environment does need to have the same love and attention that the indoor environment has and should not be seen as just a space to play.

It would be good practice for Year 1 staff to go and look at Year R environments to see the areas that they have set up. An engaging writing table is essential in Year 1; other areas such as small world play, role play, book corners, workshop areas are also important. Year R and Year 1 staff could work on this together.

Children should have access to independent resources such as pens, pencils, whiteboard and creative materials in the classroom, and this should be mirrored outside.

Issues to consider

When teachers are planning activities for children they should make these as practical as possible; for example, children will get from more pouring liquid into jugs and reading the measurement on the scales, as part of free play at the water table or perhaps a cookery activity than from any worksheet:

Figure 1.5 Practical maths activity

Addition	
2 + 0 =	10 + 2 =
2 + 1 =	9 + 2 =
2 + 2 =	8 + 2 =
2 + 3 =	7 + 2 =
2 + 4 =	6 + 2 =
2 + 5 =	5 + 2 =
2 + 6 =	4 + 2 =
2 + 7 =	3 + 2 =
2 + 8 =	2 + 2 =
2 + 9 =	1 + 2 =
2 + 10 =	0 + 2 =

Figure 1.6 Maths worksheet

A balance between annotated photographs and recorded work in books is manageable and supports assessment and future planning.

Children should be given opportunities to write for different purposes that link with the theme or topic, using different writing tools. It is important to remember that young children do not always need to sit at a table to write. Writing can happen outside, on the floor lying on their tummies to develop core muscles and strength, standing at a table or with a clipboard, or sharing writing on one large piece of paper. Children need to operate in a way that suits them and meets their own individual needs. We recognise that children need to learn to sit down and write using a pencil and paper but this can happen as part of a wide range of experiences in recording their ideas.

Figure 1.7 Writing for pleasure

Figure 1.8 Girl writing outdoors

Terms 5 and 6

During these terms, we need to be aware of the need to ensure a smooth transition from Year 1 to 2; however, the basic timetable doesn't change! We look to tweak the practice that has been happening on a daily basis. As discussed above, rather than having adult support at the table for writing each afternoon, the teacher should break away from this to allow children to become more independent and creative with their writing ready for Year 2 allowing the teacher to focus on a different group activity. As they develop their skills, many children will require far less adult support with their writing and should be expected to complete the bulk of their work independently.

Guided reading groups will have been introduced during the year, often as one of the teacher-focused afternoon group sessions and these can continue in Terms 5 and 6, along with regular whole-class shared reading sessions. These will foster children's skills through, for example, echo reading, predicting what will happen and responding to questions.

Each term so far will have included dedicated time for staff to deliver a phonics programme (this may vary from school to school). Children would have been assessed throughout the year and intervention put in place for children who may need it. During this term children will complete the phonics screening check. Each school will deliver this in a way that suits the needs of individual children.

At the end of term 6 a transition meeting for parents of Year 1 children moving into Year 2 should be held so that parents are aware of the expectations of Year 2.

<u>Areas for consideration</u>

- Teachers need to continue to promote spiritual, moral, social and cultural development through a range of enrichment activities (think about outside learning, trips, visitors and so on).

- Staff will need to adapt the way they organise the classroom.

- In order to achieve the best outcomes for children, staffing ratios may need to be reviewed.

- Not all Year 1 classrooms have a Year 1 outside classroom – schools may need to think creatively about this.

- Schools need to be flexible and acutely responsive to the needs of children. For some cohorts, it may be necessary to continue with EYFS provision for longer than others.

- Schools need to decide if and when to introduce guided reading sessions and how these are organised.

- Schools should consider how they will maintain a strong partnership with parents.

<u>To conclude</u>

Year 1 staff need to understand the principles behind the drive for effective transition between Year R and 1 and a shared vision needs to be the starting point (refer back to trust principles).

We need to think of an education that is going to enthuse and engage children with effective transition.

To achieve the highest levels of involvement, the practice needs to offer the children:

- Security

- Trust

- Friendships

- Independence

- Risk

- Excitement and laughter

- Responsibility

- First-hand experiences

- Long periods of uninterrupted time

- Freedom to be indoors and outdoors (however, we do recognise that this cannot be the case in all schools at the moment)

- Resources that are open-ended

- Skilled teaching – timely and appropriate to the individual

2 Rationale for change

As senior leaders in a large multi-academy trust, we were aware from first-hand observations that transition from Reception into Key Stage 1 was rarely as smooth as it should be. In almost all the schools with which we worked, there was an anxiety amongst staff, sometimes driven by some senior leaders, that as soon as children started in Year 1 it was necessary to "prepare" them for the demands of the Key Stage 1 tests. Time and again we saw teachers trying to motivate whole classes of children to write story openings or endings, to compare aspects of life now with the past or to identify the differences between cities, towns and villages (all part of the Key Stage 1 subject content for Year 1) (DfE 2013). In spite of the fact that children entering Year 1 are just five years old, classrooms lacked the vibrancy and resources of EYFS and more often resembled classrooms in Key Stage 2 with tables and chairs for each child, working walls and a distinct lack of resources for play. At the time, a great deal of the work in foundation subjects consisted of completing worksheets and the work was generally of a lower quality than children had been producing when they were in the Reception classes. Much of the Key Stage 1 curriculum in the foundation subjects is fairly abstract and activities often lacked an overall context which would have provided children with a meaningful purpose for learning. What we observed were conscientious teachers, anxious to do their best, working much harder than the children, trying to motivate them and keep them on task. Sue, one of the two authors, recalls that over many years in her career as a primary teacher, she taught every year group in the primary age range. She thoroughly enjoyed working with different age groups and seeing children develop, mature and make progress over the year; however, she had to admit that she found teaching a Year 1 class early in her career, the most challenging. With the benefit of hindsight, she recognised that her expectations were inappropriate to the age and developmental stage of the children – many children are not developmentally ready to sit at desks engaging in pencil and paper activities and as a young, inexperienced teacher, she was focusing too much on behaviour management and **what** children were learning rather than **how** they learned.

Having experienced a holistic, theme-based curriculum in the Early Years Foundation Stage, the move to a subject-based curriculum with its end of year expectations, including the Year 1 Phonics Screening Check, was interpreted by almost all schools as the time to move to a formal timetable, with English and Mathematics dominating each morning's session and foundation subjects, including Science, being taught in the afternoon. Almost universally, this was taken to mean that a whole-class approach to teaching should be implemented, with children for the most part working inside the classroom, tackling work individually. There was some evidence of paired working, especially in Mathematics, but for the majority of the day children were expected to work seated in ability groups at their tables. There is absolutely no reason why assessing children against end of year learning outcomes should be the cause of subjecting them to over-formalised academic approaches. Just because the National Curriculum sets out a number of statements and expectations for children to achieve by the end of each year, it does not mean we should abandon the approaches which have been so meaningful and appropriate for children who were motivated, curious learners in our Reception classes. Nowhere does the National Curriculum specify *how* children have to be taught in order to achieve the expected outcomes, yet in many schools there is a belief that the time for play is over once children start in Year 1.

Disadvantaged children

Disadvantaged children, in particular, are likely to be far more engaged with their learning if teachers take their interests into account. Access to a broad, experiential curriculum is vital for these children as they are likely to have had significantly fewer experiences of the world than their more affluent peers. Opportunities to see plants growing in the wild, to grow them themselves and to visit and play in the woods will give a more meaningful context to the science curriculum requirements that "Pupils should be taught to identify and name a variety of common wild and garden plants, including deciduous and evergreen trees" (DfE 2013) than labelling a worksheet with the parts of a plant ever could. Similarly, identifying and naming a variety of everyday materials and describing their properties is made purposeful if a variety of those materials are used to construct a bridge strong enough to take the weight of the Three Billy Goats Gruff. The issue with trying to teach subjects in isolation is that there is likely to be little context and those children with limited life experience will be at a further disadvantage. The Key Stage 1 Geography curriculum states children should develop knowledge about the world, the United Kingdom and their locality. This can be a very abstract concept for children who have not travelled far from their homes. Using basic geographical vocabulary to refer to key physical features including beach, cliff, coast and ocean amongst others can be fairly meaningless to children who have never been to the seaside. However, using high-quality fiction and non-fiction books about the sea will help link the learning to other subjects and put it in context. A selection of non-fiction books describing the world's seven continents and five oceans, which children are expected to know by the end of Year 2, will deal with this aspect of the Geography curriculum and after initial teacher input, can be displayed within the continuous provision alongside globes, atlases and large maps of the world.

Behaviour issues in Year 1

One of the biggest areas of concern we noticed when children started Year 1 was the labelling of a small number of children, usually boys, as behaviour problems. These same children had often been described as lively and boisterous by their teachers but because they were able to follow their own interests and play outside in Reception, their behaviour had not been a particular cause for concern. In fact, their curiosity, enthusiasm and involvement in a range of activities across the curriculum was rightly seen as a positive attitude to learning by Reception staff. However, once they were in Year 1, being made to sit still for what to them seemed to be long periods of time, was really too much for them. This change in attitudes to learning is mirrored in research carried out by NFER in 2004 which is described later in this chapter.

The contrast between children's experiences of learning in EYFS and in Year 1 was both striking and uncomfortable. As discussed in Chapter 1, our approach when schools join our Trust has been to implement a play-based curriculum in EYFS based on the characteristics of effective learning which took account of children's interests. This often took time and a significant amount of staff training – however, a strong commitment from our senior leaders to getting attitudes to learning right from the start, resulted in a consistently child-centred approach to Reception and nursery classes in all our schools. We now needed to address the issues arising from transition when children moved into Year 1 and beyond and how we set about this is described in detail in Chapters 3 and 4.

Child development theories

McDowall Clark states absolutely correctly that "The reason early learning of formal academic skills does not translate into long term gains is because formal learning tends to be too abstract for young children's development. For the first six years at a minimum, learning must be active and meaningful" (McDowall Clark 2017, p. 109).

A wealth of research into early child development confirms this. In her comprehensive synthesis of child development theories over various domains, Maria Robinson (2008) noted that children make significant jumps in development at various stages from birth to three and then again from three to five. However, from the age of five to seven, children's development tends to plateau before the next major shift round about the age of seven. She suggests this is in order to allow the child to "consolidate and improve on their previous abilities" (2008, p. 179). She also points out that it is not usually until the age of six that children are able to demonstrate finer control over writing tasks because, before then, their wrist bones are not fully developed and it is not till the age of seven that a mature grasp for holding pencils, brushes and using scissors skilfully is consistently evident. (This is in spite of the fact that the Early Learning Goal for moving and handling – the expectation by the end of the Reception year –states that children should be able to handle equipment and tools effectively including pencils for writing!)

There is broad agreement amongst many researchers (Bredekamp 1987; Tassoni 2007 quoted in Fisher 2010) that round about the age of seven as children come to the end of Year 2, they are able to work in a more abstract way. In her book, *Moving on to Key Stage 1* (Fisher 2010), which although written over 10 years ago, is still relevant to this issue, Julie Fisher refers to the lack of information in literature on child development between the ages of 5 and 6. She comes to the conclusion this is because there are few significant differences in the way children of this age learn. Given there is so little evidence of any major developmental shift between a five- and a six-year-old, common sense would appear to indicate that the approach which works best for a five-year-old will also be successful for a six-year-old and beyond.

Approaches to teaching and learning across the United Kingdom

Scotland

It is interesting to note that throughout the United Kingdom, it is only in England that there is this move to a more formal way of working as children move into Year 1. The Scottish education system specifically states it defines Early Years as pre-birth to eight years old and that many aspects of the Scottish Early Years Framework (2008) are equally relevant to children beyond the age of eight. This framework states: "Play is central to how children learn, both in terms of cognitive skills and softer skills around relating to other people. It is a fundamental part of children's quality of life and a right enshrined in the UN Convention on the Rights of the Child." The curriculum for children in Scotland (which covers the ages from 3 to 18) is set out in its *Curriculum for Excellence* (2008). In setting out principles and practices for each broad curriculum area, it advocates a mix of appropriate approaches for all – those for literacy and English include:

- the use of relevant, real-life and enjoyable contexts which build upon children and young people's own experiences

- effective direct and interactive teaching

- a balance of spontaneous play and planned activities

- harnessing the motivational benefits of following children and young people's interests through responsive planning

- collaborative working and independent thinking and learning

- making meaningful links for learners across different curriculum areas

- building on the principles of Assessment is for Learning

- the development of problem-solving skills and approaches

Each of these statements sits very comfortably with what we know about how young children learn – how refreshing to see this approach promoted way beyond the Early Years' curriculum.

Wales

In Wales, the Early Years phase is defined as the period of life from pre-birth to the end of Foundation Phase or 0 to 7 years of age. From September 2008, the Welsh Assembly Government introduced a new Foundation Phase for children from 3 to 7 years of age, combining early years education for 3- to 5-year-olds and Key Stage 1 of the National Curriculum for 5- to 7-year-olds. The Foundation Phase places a greater emphasis on active, experiential learning. The Welsh government is currently consulting on a completely new curriculum which will be in place from 2022. The article "Education Is Changing" on the Welsh government website (Welsh Government 2019) confirms that the principles of the Foundation Phase will remain, but that they will become a part of one seamless curriculum for children aged 3 to 16, providing more joined-up learning. It intends to remove Key Stages 2, 3 and 4 and states that the way children are taught will change, with a greater emphasis on skills and experience rather than just knowledge. The reason for this is because the Welsh government recognises that the curriculum must prepare young people to thrive in a future where digital skills, adaptability and creativity – alongside knowledge – are crucial. A report from the Public Policy Institute for Wales (2017) states that: "Given the scale and pace of change, it is likely that many children in primary school today will work in jobs that either do not exist today, or at least have constituent tasks that are very different from those of today" (Bell et al., 2017).

Northern Ireland

The Foundation Stage in Northern Ireland represents the beginning of the compulsory stage of education for children in primary school. Children who have attained the age of 4 on or before 1 July start primary school at the beginning of the September that year. The Foundation Stage curriculum applies to children in Year 1 and Year 2 of primary school. The Northern Ireland education department has developed a curriculum which uses play as the context for learning. Its publication *Learning to Learn* (Northern Ireland 2013) recognises that stimulation through play is an important factor in the social, emotional and educational development of the child.

The impact of regular standardised testing on teaching methods

So it is clear that throughout the United Kingdom, it is still only in England that there is an expectation in many schools that children should move to a more formal way of working at the age of five. However, other countries still retain a focus on regular standardised testing which impacts on the way children are taught. This is particularly the case in the USA, where students take an average of 112 standardised tests from pre-kindergarten to Grade 12. In their book, *Let the Children Play*, Sahlberg and Doyle (2019) tell of an encounter in a New York park with a teacher who laments the lack of play in her school as a result not just of the imposition of a barrage of standardised tests but also of parents' lack of understanding of the crucial importance of play. In an attempt to ensure they secure entry into the school of their choice, many parents attempt to drill their three-year-old children in early literacy and numeracy skills, whilst play as a vehicle for problem solving, developing concentration and discovery is seen as trivial and unimportant.

The impact of age on starting school

Throughout much of the wider world, children do not start school until the age of six or seven and there are numerous studies which suggest that children are not generally disadvantaged by a later start to formal schooling. One recent example is that of Estonia, a small Baltic state. The Organisation for Economic Co-operation and Development (OECD) recently published the Programme for International Student Assessment (PISA) results for 2018. (OECD 2019). PISA is a triennial international survey which measures 15-year-olds' ability to use their reading, Mathematics and science knowledge and skills to meet real-life challenges.

In PISA 2018, Estonian students ranked first among European countries in all three domains of assessment. It was also placed first in Reading and Science and third in Mathematics among the OECD countries. Estonia ranks fifth in Reading, fourth in Science and eighth in Mathematics among all participating countries and economies. By comparison, the UK was ranked 14th in Reading and Science and 18th in Mathematics.

The Estonian education department (Republic of Estonia Ministry of Education and Research 2020), in its explanation of why the results were so high, attributed "almost universal access to quality early education" as a key factor in students' success. Children in Estonia do not start school formally until they are seven years old, but almost all children attend a pre-school educational establishment. Pre-school education consists of child-oriented active learning methods, including language immersion, discovery learning and outdoor learning. Supporting each child's individuality, creativity and learning through play are seen as paramount. In the article "Estonia, Early Childhood Education and Care" (Eurydice 2019), the purpose of pre-school education is seen to support children's integral development and readiness for school. In order to achieve this, there is a focus on the "physical, mental, social and emotional development of the child in order that the child develops a comprehensive and positive self-image, understanding of the surrounding environment, ethical behaviour and initiative, first working habits, physical activity and understanding of the importance of maintaining health, and playing, learning, social and personal skills." These are the attributes seen to be important and impacting on future academic and personal success and which form the basis of the information passed on when children start school; there are no formal tests or assessments.

Early formal learning and children's well-being and mental health

In her review of different countries' policies regarding the age at which children start school, McDowall Clark (2017) quotes research from Browning and Heinesen (2007) and Elder (2010) when she states, "Young children who begin formal schooling before they are developmentally mature are more at risk of mental health problems and the younger children start school, the more likely they are to be diagnosed with Attention Deficit Hyperactive Disorder. This is because starting school later provides greater opportunities for the sort of playful learning that supports young children's communication skills, disposition towards learning and ability to regulate their own behaviour, whereas anxiety, lack of self-esteem and poor motivation are all associated with formal demands at too young an age" (McDowall Clark 2017). Our five- and six-year-old children have already been in school for over a year and so we clearly cannot do anything about the age at which they start. However, the reference to playful learning which builds on the *Characteristics of Effective Learning* (set out in the Statutory Framework for the Early Years Foundation Stage, DfE 2018) is something we can, and should, all put in place.

The government report *Children and young people's mental health—the role of education: Government Response to the First Joint Report of the Education and Health Committees of Session* (2016–17) looks to schools as well as the health service to promote strong mental health. By continuing with the principles that underpin effective Early Years practice, we can continue to build children's self-esteem and self-motivation as they move into Year 1 and beyond in an environment that recognises and values individual strengths and needs whilst at the same time supporting children to understand the needs of others. It is encouraging to see that the government is looking to the education system to promote mental health; by continuing to build on the principles of the EYFS, and ensuring children's Personal, Social and Emotional Development underpins our curriculum, our Year 1 children should continue to thrive.

Given recent concerns about children's well-being and the importance of fostering strong mental health we were interested in the research by Dee and Sievertson who noted that in Denmark, children typically enrol in school during the calendar year in which they turn six. Their research showed that "a one-year delay in the start of school dramatically reduces inattention/hyperactivity at age 7 (effect size = −0.7), a measure of self-regulation with strong negative links to student achievement" (Dee and Sievertson 2015).

Sahlberg and Doyle (2019) argue convincingly that play is vitally important in the lives of young children and essential to the healthy development of their minds and bodies. They show how play supports children's emotional development by enabling them to explore their personal feelings and ideas and to develop empathy by learning how others feel and think. They cite the vital role of play in cultivating the complex personal and social skills children need to make their way in the world. They make the point that in many countries (not just England), play is being eroded because of a plethora of standardised tests intended to demonstrate academic achievement. They argue passionately that: "Every moment of play that is abolished from school, every recess that is cancelled, every machine that replaces a caring qualified teacher and every unnecessary, high stress standardised test that is forced upon a child represents a theft from children who yearn for movement, creativity, discovery, joy, warmth, encouragement and friendship as they learn and grow" (Sahlberg and Doyle 2019, p. 8).

Research on transition from Reception into Year 1

Back in 2004, Sharp et al., a team of researchers working with the National Foundation for Educational Research, carried out a detailed study of parents', teachers' and children's reactions to transition from Reception into KS1 in their document *Making a Successful Transition to Year 1* (NFER 2004). This research included a telephone survey of teachers in 60 English schools. It includes a frequently quoted response from two boys about their experiences in Year 1. The boys noted there were fewer opportunities to work with friends, move around freely and go outside. When the researchers asked whether there was anything they did not like about being in Year 1, the most common response was that they disliked spending time sitting still, on the carpet, listening to the teacher.

- Researcher: Is there anything you don't like about being in Year 1?

- First Boy: Being on the carpet for a long time.

- Second Boy: Neither do I because it's very boring.

- First Boy: And it wastes our time playing.

- Second Boy: It wastes your life.

(NFER 2004)

The Ofsted report on the Foundation Stage (as it was then) (Ofsted 2006) noted transition was an issue for many schools and, in 2009, the final report of the Independent Review of the Primary Curriculum (Department for Children, Schools and Families (DCSF) 2009) stated that "some aspects of the EYFS should be extended into the primary curriculum … including social and emotional areas of development and widening the curriculum opportunities for child-initiated and play-based activity." Yet over ten years on, the majority of schools still see Year 1 as the time to begin a formal approach to learning.

ONE SCHOOL'S EXPERIENCE

At Pickhurst Infant Academy in Bromley, the headteacher and senior staff were concerned that there was a dip in the proportion of children in Year 1 working at age-related expectations, especially in writing, compared to their attainment at the end of EYFS. They knew staff in the year group were committed, capable teachers but children were not demonstrating the same levels of achievement as they had been. They were worried that some children who had been happily settled in Reception were tearful and reluctant to come into school in the mornings. Some parents were also complaining that their children were unhappy. Staff at the school looked at the research commissioned by Blackpool Council in the **Blackpool Transition Project Reception to Year 1** (Blackpool Council 2012). Researchers in the Blackpool project used a series of measures in which a set of scales describe levels of children's well-being and involvement. Each scale has five levels ranging from level 1 – extremely low to level 5, extremely high. Of the four schools involved in the Blackpool project, each was asked to choose six Reception children at the beginning of the project and carry out a Wellbeing and Involvement assessment on them using these scales. They were then reassessed on the same scales in the first three weeks in Year 1. Researchers noted that 98% of children had dropped at least one scale point with some dropping up to four scale points. Staff at Pickhurst Infant Academy recognised that the findings from this research were mirrored in their own observations; when transition was not smooth and children moved from a play-based EYFS to a formal Year 1 setting, learning was impeded children because children were uncomfortable and disengaged. Staff at the school took the decision to abandon their traditional approach to teaching in Year 1 and instead looked back to the principles underpinning the approach to teaching and learning in the EYFS; that every child is unique and that each child learns and develops in different ways and at different rates, the importance of positive relationships and of enabling environments. They also recognised that their approach needed to build on the Characteristics of Effective Learning – which can be summarised as playing and exploring, active, "hands-on" learning and creating and thinking critically. They implemented a strategy where each Year 1 teacher was "buddied" with an EYFS teacher in order to help Year 1 teachers understand the principles and methodology of child-initiated, play-based learning. This proved highly effective in promoting dialogue and a shared understanding of the factors that impact on young children's learning. Over the last three years, the school has developed a curriculum in Year 1 in which children are encouraged to follow their own interests in a rich, stimulating environment, which supports and challenges children. Specific skills and knowledge are taught in a mixture of whole-class, small group and individual sessions. Challenging perceptions of what teaching should look like in Year 1 has not always been easy and has required investment in staff training, regular communication and partnership with parents as well as significant support from senior leaders. However, the rewards have been worth the investment, with staff confident they know how to move children's learning on through modelling, questioning and accurate assessment and children who are happy, curious and interested.

Summary

Effective transition from Reception into Year 1 has been of concern for many years and we have seen this is particularly an issue affecting schools in England, compared to the rest of the United Kingdom. Research into child development suggests that there is little difference in the way most five- and six-year olds learn, yet many schools still believe that children in Year 1 need a formal curriculum. There are clear implications for children's mental health and well-being if transition is too abrupt and inappropriate for five-year olds.

REFLECTION

- What is transition like in your school?

- What is effective and what would you like to improve?

- How can you ensure your transition arrangements promote children's mental health?

- How can we build in meaningful opportunities for play into the curriculum?

References

Bell, M., Bristow, D. and Martin, S. (2017) *The Future of Work in Wales, Public Policy Institute for Wales*. Available at https://www.gov.wales (Accessed 7 August 2019).

Blackpool Council (2012) *Blackpool Transition Project*, ISBN: 1-85838-720-5.

Bredekamp, S. (Ed.). (1987). *Developmentally Appropriate Practice in Early Child-hood Programs Serving Children from Birth through Age 8*. Washington, DC: National Association for the Education of Young Children.

Browning, M. and Heinesen, E. (2007) Class size, teacher hours and educational attainment, *The Scandinavian Journal of Economics*, 109(2): 415–438.

Dee, T. and Sievertson, H. (2015) *The Gift of Time? School Starting Age and Mental Health*, National Bureau of Economic Research Working paper no 2160. Cambridge MA: NBER.

Department for Children, Schools and Families (DCSF) (2009) *Independent Review of the Primary Curriculum*, DCSF-00499-2009. London: DCSF.

Department for Education (2018) *Statutory Framework for the Early Years Foundation Stage*. Available at https://www.gov.uk/government/publications/early-years-foundation-stage-framework--2 (Accessed 11 March 2019).

Department for Education (DfE) (2013) *The National Curriculum in England*, DfE-00177-2013. London: DfE.

Education and Health committee, HC451, published 24 October 2017 by the authority of the House of Commons.

Elder, T.E. (2010) The Importance of Relative Standards in ADHD diagnoses: evidence based on exact birth dates, *Journal of Health Economics*, 29(5): 641–656

Eurydice (2019) *Estonia – Early Childhood Education and Care*. Available at https://eacea.ec.europa.eu/national-policies/eurydice/content/early-childhood-education-and-care-24_en (Accessed 4 May 2020).

Fisher, J. (2010) *Moving on to Key Stage 1*. Maidenhead: Open University Press.

McDowall Clark, R. (2017) *Exploring the Contexts for Early Learning*. Oxford: Routledge.

Northern Ireland Government (2013) *Learning to Learn – A Framework for Early Years Education and Learning*. Available at www.ni.gov.uk (Accessed 14 August 2019).

Ofsted (2006) *The Foundation Stage: A Survey of 144 Settings*. London: Ofsted.

Organisation for Economic Co-operation and Development (OECD) (2019) *PISA 2018 Results* (Vol. I). Available at https://www.oecd-ilibrary.org (Accessed 4 May 2020).

Republic of Estonia Ministry of Education and Research (2020) *PISA*. Available at www.hm.ee/sites/default/files/pisa_2018_english_summary_ed.pdf (Accessed 3 May 2020).

Robinson, M. (2008) *Child Development from Birth to Eight*. Maidenhead: Open University Press.

Sahlberg, P. and Doyle, W. (2019) *Let the Children Play*. New York: Oxford University Press.

Scottish Government (2008) *Curriculum for Excellence: Building the Curriculum 3: A Framework for Learning and Teaching*. Edinburgh: Scottish Government.

Sharp, C., White, G., Burge, B. and Eames, A. (2004) *Making a Successful Transition to Year 1*, Practical Research for Education 35, May 2006, pp. 20–27. Slough: NFER.

Tassoni, P. (2007) *Child Development 6–16 years*. Oxford: Heinemann.

Welsh Government (2019) *Education Is Changing*. Available at https://www.gov.wales/ (Accessed 7 August 2019).

3 Enabling environments

The environment is a fundamental element of effective Year 1 provision. We know that children learn and develop well in enabling environments in which stimulating resources and experiences are planned to meet individual needs and there is a strong partnership between teachers, parents and carers. Children thrive when relationships within the school are positive.

In an ideal situation, Year 1, like the Early Years Foundation Stage (EYFS), will have its own identity within a school where the leadership team actively encourage and support the staff, empowering them to build upon practical learning, helping children develop independence by making their own choices about resources and activities and choosing whether these take place indoors or outside.

When children leave EYFS they often leave a spacious, vibrant classroom with an outside learning area. Classrooms in EYFS rarely have 30 tables and chairs; instead, there is usually a wide range of tactile, hands-on activities based on the seven areas of learning. These promote independence and provide an environment where children show high levels of well-being and involvement. In many schools, EYFS classrooms have openings for children to free flow between classrooms where up to 120 children can mix and work together.

In some schools we have observed children walking into classrooms in Year 1 which look little different from classrooms in Years 4 or 5, where they are expected to sit at tables and chairs all day, where resources are handed to them and there is no ownership of the room.

When children have been used to a sense of excitement and expectation, on entering their EYFS classrooms each morning, because those rooms have been set up to promote curiosity, awe and wonder, it is no wonder that children sometimes revert to passivity, occasionally displaying low-level poor behaviour with little spark or enthusiasm for learning. This is something that can be distressing for both teachers and parents when children had always demonstrated enthusiasm on entering their classroom each morning, eager to get started on the activities and keen to find out what the day ahead would bring.

So what do our Year 1 classrooms look like?

Indoors, we might have tables and chairs for up to twelve children, so up to two groups of six or three groups of four children could be working with or without an adult at any one time. There will be an attractive, well-stocked book corner, with the core text prominently displayed. We have found that having four or five copies of the core text alongside a big book of the same text and a display of small world characters and resources, linked to the text, is really effective in drawing children in to retell the story.

Figure 3.1 Planning the classroom environment around a core text

Figure 3.2 Planning the classroom environment around a core text

Enabling environments 43

Figure 3.3 Planning the classroom environment around a core text

Figure 3.4 Planning the classroom environment around a core text

Children's learning can be developed further by having a role play area alongside and a writing area where children can access a range of materials and writing implements. This writing area can be a sheet of paper stretched across a table or rolled out along the floor (children love lying on their tummies to write). Blank booklets and leaflets, as well as different colours, sizes and shapes of paper, will be available. We always have a large workshop area where children are free to junk model, draw, paint, glue, stick and explore a variety of media. Again, all resources are organised so that children can access these independently. Depending on children's interests we might also have a builder's tray with some sort of malleable material, some construction, mathematical activities linked to the focus of the Mathematics being taught at the time and one or two investigation areas, which might be linked to the topic, or reflect something children are interested in. Some of our schools also have a display of WOW words which extend children's vocabulary and capture their imagination. In a topic on "Superheroes," the teacher's list of "WOW" words included "mystifying, ominous, powerful, colossal" – all words children loved to use in their writing. The photographs below give examples of the sorts of activities children have enjoyed exploring and investigating.

Figure 3.5 Rainforest investigation area

Enabling environments 45

Figure 3.6 Owl Babies, small world play and writing opportunities

Figure 3.7 Chinese New Year

The role play area in Year 1

The role play area is an important part of the learning environment for young children and teachers need to plan how to develop the skills children have acquired in the Reception class. In Istead Rise Primary School in north-west Kent, one of the Swale Academies Trust schools, the role play area is seen as a key area for building on children's speaking and listening skills. Recognising that being able to speak clearly and confidently in public is an important skill, Karen, the teacher, makes a stage available in the role play area and encourages children to practise speaking and performing in front of others. With this approach, children can continue to build on the skills they have already developed in the role play area, some of which include interactive dialogue, using imagination, communicating ideas and thoughts, improvisation, and taking on different roles. However, setting the expectations and giving children opportunities to develop their confidence in speaking in front of an audience will help them meet the requirements of the National Curriculum programmes of study for spoken language, some of which include "speak audibly and fluently with an increasing command of Standard English" and "participating in performances role-play and improvisations" (DfE 2013). In some of our school, teachers add prompts for adults as can be seen in the photograph of a role play café.

Figure 3.8 Role play café

Making the most of an outdoor learning area

Ideally, children should also have access to an outdoor area, although we recognise that this is something not all schools have readily available. However, with some negotiation and forward planning it is usually possible in most schools to identify an area which can be developed for outdoor learning in Year 1. Children love to be outside exploring and investigating. Our experience shows most children display high levels of involvement and engagement and are happy when learning outside. Each child is unique and each develops and learns in different ways and at different rates; they flourish in different situations and it is important that we continue to recognise this and offer children an appropriate environment where they feel comfortable and confident. Assuming space is available, there is absolutely no reason why children should not be allowed to choose to complete their work inside or outside.

Figure 3.9 Three boys working together

Where schools have direct access to an outdoor area, this needs to be as high-profile as the inside environment. For this to happen staff need to invest fully in the importance of an outside area and understand the high-quality learning that can happen when children are outside. That being said, we recognise an outside area can be time-consuming. Staff need to plan effectively for the space and encourage children to tidy up after themselves and take ownership. It is not just a space for children to run around in, it is a space to focus children and bring the learning from indoors, outside. It should have the same love and attention as the indoor environment and be seen as an outside classroom. Resources can be left outside and sheds or containers can be set up for children to access resources independently. Schools will need to work out how best to organise the setting up of the outdoor area; in our schools, staff get the indoor area ready the night before and the outdoor area ready first thing in the morning.

So what does the outdoor area in a Year 1 environment look like?

Even within our own schools, the outdoor areas differ hugely from school to school; some have a small courtyard area; others a huge space with tarmac, grass and growing areas. But however much space is available the underlying principles remain the same. The outdoor area should be an extension of the classroom. When planning how to set up the Year 1 outside area, teachers will find it helpful to seek support from staff in Reception, who know the children well. It is important to remember that cohorts vary from year to year and activities that are really popular with one group may not be so attractive to another. Year 1 staff should find out what areas did the children use the most in Reception and then find ways of incorporating those activities into their outside area. They also need to identify gaps in the learning of specific cohorts or groups and plan to address these outside as well as indoors.

It is important to ensure writing opportunities are planned for with all activities; this could be chalks on the floor, whiteboards and pens, clipboards and paper or writing tool kits for children to pick up and take wherever they would like. Prompts to support independent writing should be available.

The beauty of learning outside means things can be large scale. Junk modelling can happen with huge boxes, large pieces of paper can be pinned onto the walls for painting and other art work, a large stage can be built (to keep costs down, this can be built with pallets), to encourage role play, large mathematical resources can be used within the natural environment and builders' trays, sometimes referred to as "tuff spots" can be used for messy play and small world play.

Figure 3.10 Maths outdoors

Figure 3.11 Maths outdoors

Resources should be available for children to access independently and put away independently to support with teacher workload. Children can squeeze paint out of paint bottles themselves and mix paint to create new colours – none of this needs to be pre-squeezed into pots for children. Teachers just need to ensure resources are replenished when they are running out. Local businesses will always donate things for outside areas, such as pallets, old tyres for seating and crates. It is important to use real life objects so if children are engaging in construction role play, they need to have real bricks to use and try out different materials to make their own cement.

Having an outside area means that physical development can be encouraged in this space. Some schools may have fixed apparatus that the children can use, but if that is not available, there are plenty of activities that can be planned for outside with different equipment to support physical development as well as meeting the requirements of the National Curriculum PE end of year objectives. Ball skills can be encouraged, along with target throwing with bean bags. Children can create their own obstacle courses using equipment that is available; all of these activities support hand–eye co-ordination and developing of the core muscles which children need to be able to sit and write. If possible, water and sand play should be encouraged in Year 1. This will not mirror Reception, but teachers can extend this type of play now the children have moved into Year 1. Large water tables or water channelling systems provide a wealth of opportunities to learn not just about capacity and floating and sinking, but also ways of transporting water, how to increase and decrease the flow of water and the properties of materials, including waterproof and not waterproof, absorbent and not absorbent, and opaque and transparent. These are all included in the Year 1 Science curriculum. If water play is available all the time, children can revisit these concepts and deepen and embed their understanding,

At Peel Clothworkers' School on the Isle of Man, Year 1 teachers were able to consolidate children's understanding of grids, by setting up an activity in the sand pit. Strips of masking tape were used to form gridlines across the sand pit. One side was labelled with letters and the other with numbers. Children had to describe the location of objects hidden in the sand by using the correct grid reference. They were also able to use the grid to order and arrange combinations of objects in patterns and sequences.

rather than relying on a short sequence of lessons focusing on the simple physical properties of a variety of everyday materials.

Not all children like the hustle and bustle of a busy outside area so it is important to plan for a quiet space where children might like to take their writing tools kits or sit and share a text. Books should be available for children to use, but these need to be the correct level and in good condition. Making a "library shed" is an effective way of having access to books outside and keeping them in good condition.

Disadvantaged children

We were keen to see how our provision impacted on disadvantaged children, in terms of both their engagement and motivation and their achievement. We carried out a small-scale action research project to identify what sorts of activities interested disadvantaged children when they had access to continuous provision, with no adult direction. Over the course of a week or so, we carried out targeted observations of these children and analysed the time they spent at different activities. We noted they gravitated towards the outdoor learning area, and in particular to water play. We carried out a resource audit of these areas and thought about how we could increase the learning opportunities provided by water play, in particular to support mathematical and writing development, as well as science. We ordered new water channelling equipment, water trays, some more tuff spots, hose pipe attachments, jugs, buckets, funnels and pipettes. We also ensured there was an adult close by who was able to use effective questioning to help children explore, investigate and solve problems. Writing opportunities were planned for this area and we also added water play to other areas outside to try to encourage them to use the different areas. We noticed children quickly gained confidence in using mathematical vocabulary as they explored the range of resources available. The information we gained from these observations was invaluable in that teachers were able to use their knowledge of what intrigued and fascinated these children when planning activities.

Recording work

Many teachers have asked us how much recorded work children should do in Year 1 and what exercise books should be used. There is no right or wrong answer to this. It is worth discussing with colleagues and senior leaders the purpose and value of recording work. Indeed, the practice of using photographs to record children's achievements as is common in EYFS provision, could continue certainly for the first term and it is important to value children's writing across the independent learning activities made available within the continuous provision. In Rockmount Primary School, each child has a free writing book. All other work is stored in a lever arch file, where work in English, Mathematics and foundation subjects is stored in three separate sections with the most recent work at the front. This immediately gives information on progress and coverage. Feedback to children is immediate – there is no marking. Much of the work in Mathematics is recorded on annotated photographs. The co-head explained that although it takes longer for staff to set up activities, there is no marking and the benefits are children who are engaged, focused and demonstrating independence.

In Westlands Primary School, English and Mathematics exercise books are introduced in terms 3 and 4. Before then, samples of children's work are kept in folders along with annotated photographs as is the case in EYFS. Many schools are finding it helpful to have class books for foundation subjects, rather than every child having a History, Geography and RE book for example.

Summary

In order to support a smooth transition, classroom environments in Year 1 should resemble those of EYFS as much as possible. We recognise that in some schools senior leaders might not understand the importance of continuing to provide opportunities for children to learn outdoors and it may be necessary to negotiate and articulate the benefits. Your biggest advocates are often children themselves!

REFLECTION

We have discussed the importance of a stimulating, well-organised classroom environment for our Year 1 children.

How well does your classroom:

- Provide stimulation and challenge

- Reflect children's interests

- Celebrate learning

- Provide independent accessible resources

- Encourage children's creativity and problem solving

- Encourage independence and help children develop a positive attitude towards learning?

Reference

Department for Education (DfE) (2013) *The National Curriculum in England*, reference DfE-00178-2013. London: DfE.

4 **Putting ideas into practice**

As discussed in Chapter 2, we strongly believe that the principles underpinning the Early Years Foundation Stage (EYFS) curriculum are equally relevant to older children and that children in Year 1 need to continue to experience a child-centred, play-based curriculum which reflects their interests and which builds upon their prior attainment. However, we recognise that is easier said than done and this chapter sets out in detail how we have gone about that.

Building on prior learning

In any Year 1 class, there are likely to be children who did not achieve a Good Level of Development (GLD) at the end of EYFS. To support continuity of learning from EYFS it is strongly recommended that Year 1 staff are involved in moderation at the end of EYFS. Teachers should moderate assessments together and agree judgements and Year 1 teachers need to be able to interpret the EYFS data in order to plan effectively. Year 1 staff should also know that children who did not achieve a GLD might have met the expected standards in reading, writing and Mathematics. EYFS profile results are often lower for disadvantaged and for summer-born children; those with English as an additional language may not yet have developed the skills to demonstrate they have met the expectations in communication and language, reading or writing. If possible, Reception teachers should support Year 1 colleagues with the first week of planning as they know the children, their interests and abilities. We have found it helpful, in monitoring children's progress for Year 1 staff, to re-assess in October and then again at Christmas, any children who did not achieve a GLD at the end of EYFS. This should be shared with leaders and the Special Educational Needs Co-ordinator (SENDCo) or Inclusion lead in the school in case extra provision needs to be put in place.

Engagement	Motivation	Thinking
Playing and exploring	**Active Learning**	**Creative and Critical Thinking**
Finding out and exploring • Showing curiosity about objects, events and people • Using senses to explore the world around them • Engaging in open-ended activity • Showing particular interests	***Being involved and concentrating*** • Maintaining focus on their activity for a period of time • Showing high levels of energy, fascination • Not easily distracted • Paying attention to details	***Having their own ideas*** • Thinking of ideas • Finding ways to solve problems • Finding new ways to do things
Playing with what they know • Pretending objects are things from their experience • Representing their experiences in play • Taking on a role in their play • Acting out experiences with other people	***Keeping on trying*** • Persisting with activity when challenges occur • Showing a belief that more effort or a different approach will pay off • Bouncing back after difficulties	***Making links*** • Making links and noticing patterns in their experience • Making predictions • Testing their ideas • Developing ideas of grouping, sequences, caues and effect
Being willing to 'have a go' • Initiating activities • Seeking challenges • Showing a can do attitude • taking a risk, engaging in new experiences and learning by trial and error	***Enjoying achieving what they set out to do*** • Showing satisfaction in meeting their own goals • Being proud of how they accomplished something- not just the end result • Enjoying meeting challenges for their own sake rather than external rewards or praise	***Choosing ways to do things*** • Planning, making decisions about how to approach a task, solve a problem and reach a goal • Checking how well their activities are going • Changing strategy as needed • Reviewing how well the approach worked

Figure 4.1 Characteristics of effective learning

The Early Years Foundation Stage Handbook (2018) states that as well as data, "the Characteristics of Effective Learning narratives will give teachers significant details about each child's learning and development. The narratives must feature in conversations between practitioners and teachers." This will form part of the transition handover.

In order to continue to develop resilience, independence and reflection, the Characteristics of Effective Learning, which are fundamental to the approach to learning and development, should continue to underpin learning across Year 1 and beyond (Figure 4.1).

How is the school day organised?

It is easy to forget that starting in Year 1 often means a number of changes for children, apart from the obvious things such as a new classroom, new teachers and a move to a subject-based curriculum. Schools are likely to have different arrangements for entering the school building- children might have to leave their parents and carers at the gate to line up on the playground with older children, they will have regular playtimes, they may have to ask to go to the toilet, arrangements for lunchtimes might be different. Some schools expect Year 1 children to attend all whole-school assemblies, though this is something we would not advocate at the beginning of the year. These issues with transition and the impact they can have are discussed more fully in Chapter 6.

Given these changes, we believe that (staffing levels and the physical environment permitting) during the first few weeks of Term 1, children should continue to experience a similar timetable to the one with which they are familiar. We recognise this may not be possible in all schools because of constraints of space, teacher knowledge, experience and confidence in implementing an Early Years' curriculum and expectations of senior leaders. However, it is really important that those first few days in Year 1 are spent getting to know the children, letting them play, observing them and introducing them to their new classroom environment. Time spent in those first few days modelling how to use the different areas of the classroom, setting out expectations of using and looking after classroom equipment, putting things away in their right place (ideally negotiated with children during those first few days) and learning the systems and routines will be time well spent.

As soon as the children are settled and have made positive relationships with their new teachers, a slightly more traditional timetable (outlined below) can be introduced. In our schools, this has generally meant a focus on English and Mathematics in the mornings and foundation subjects in the afternoons whilst still maintaining the principles of EYFS and Characteristics of Effective Learning. We recognise this approach will not suit everyone and we are reviewing our practice constantly; however, by refusing to compromise on maintaining a playful approach to learning and adopting a mixture of whole-class, small group and child- and adult-initiated learning we have found children are able to transition happily into a more traditional timetable. This is often reassuring for senior leaders who like to be able to identify when specific subjects are being taught!

When planning topics for Year 1 the question to think about is: how can we consider the children's interests and match the curriculum to the child? We have seen this work well by Year 1 teachers working closely with the Reception class teacher, children expressing what they have enjoyed learning in Reception or sharing ideas on transition days in the summer term before children start in Year 1. Some of our EYFS teachers ask the children to draw a picture and write what they have enjoyed whilst in the Reception class and send it to their new class teacher; children are then reassured they are being listened to and that their new teachers will know something about them. Some examples are provided in Chapter 6. Disadvantaged children, in particular, are likely to be far more engaged with their learning if teachers take their interests into account. Noting that the disadvantaged children in one of our cohorts gravitated towards the outdoor area and, in particular, the water play, we resourced that area so we could meet as many as possible of the objectives across the wider curriculum.

In several of our schools we have used the following timetable, which has proved to be highly successful. This timetable is implemented once the children are fully settled and ready to move on from the EYFS timetable. Some academic years it might start within two weeks of term, in others it might not start until October half-term.

Session 1 – Early morning work (15 minutes)

Children self-register as they enter the classroom and settle to early morning work. This session provides an opportunity for children to consolidate previously taught skills, fine motor control activities or targeted intervention for small groups. It is also a good time to set up memorable experiences when introducing a new topic – for example, dinosaur footprints could lead to the discovery of a dinosaur egg. Other activities could include using tweezers to pick up small objects for those children needing to develop their fine motor skills, construction activities, small world play to retell a story and a display of books about dinosaurs. There is an informal, relaxed start to the day; it gives teachers a chance to settle children and speak to parents and carers if needed. This is really important as parents would have had daily opportunities to talk to staff in EYFS and we should continue to develop this partnership and foster this important link between home and school.

Session 2 – Phonics (20–25 minutes)

We have taken a pragmatic approach to the teaching of phonics, recognising it as one component of the complex skills and processes involved in learning to read. Children will be assessed at the end of the year against the Phonics Screening Check and so we have short, regular daily phonics sessions which are interactive, fun and tailored to children's prior knowledge and skills. In our larger schools we sometimes group the children across the year group into smaller, more focused groups, although this is something we are currently reviewing. As our children are introduced to phonics in EYFS, it is familiar to them, thus supporting the transition process.

Session 3 – English (45 minutes to an hour)

It is important to understand that having an English lesson lasting for 45 minutes to an hour does not mean that all Year 1 children have to be working on an adult-directed activity for the whole session. Our English lessons consist of a mixture of whole-class, small group and adult- and child-initiated learning. We have found that the most successful approach to this is to base lessons around a high-quality core text which is shared with the class. This text, which would link to the overarching topic for the term, can be read at the beginning of the week and then explored in detail with the children. A big book or the text shared on the interactive whiteboard would be the best way to do this. During the week the children would learn specific skills and build up to a piece of writing. At the start of the year, this session would look very different from how it would by the end of the year. Towards the beginning of the year there is far more small group work with other children accessing independent learning activities than towards the end of the year. In our schools we do not introduce English exercise books until after Christmas as the majority of work is practical and we like to explore different ways for children to record their work. So, for example, if children are retelling the story of "The Three Little Pigs" we would encourage them to make blank books from pink or brown paper. We would model how to design a front cover and a "blurb" at the back and encourage children to make their own books rather than just rewrite a story in an exercise book.

Guided reading groups can be introduced during the year, often as one of the teacher-focused afternoon group sessions and these can continue in Terms 5 and 6 along with regular whole-class shared reading sessions. These will foster children's skills, for example, through echo reading, predicting what will happen and responding to questions. Teachers should determine the specific reading skills to be covered and plan to teach these ideally in the context of a core text. Year 1 children will need to experience some form of shared reading every day, which will include a focus on teaching specific reading skills and also a dedicated story time.

English lessons are not about children just sitting on the carpet listening and responding to the teacher. Communication and Language needs to be key throughout these sessions to ensure the children are forming accurate sentences verbally and learning new vocabulary. It is really important to ensure the children are able to retell the core text through role play and small world play. This gives children the time to converse with one another and share ideas. This is particularly important for children for whom English is an additional language and for those whose speaking skills are underdeveloped. Access to continuous provision is an important part of English sessions giving adults opportunities to take a genuine interest in what children are doing, to model accurate sentence structure and extend children's vocabulary. The other important point to note is that it is not necessary for all groups to cover the same learning objectives every day; it is more helpful to look at the objectives to be covered over a sequence of learning and spread those objectives over a number of days.

What does this look like in practice?

We are going to use the book *Chalk*, (Thomson, 2010) written by Bill Thomson, as an example of an English session that might be held towards the beginning of the year. This is a wordless picture book about three children who visit the park on a rainy day and who use magic chalk to draw pictures that come to life. This book was chosen as part of an overall theme of dinosaurs, which was a topic that had sparked children's interest.

Independent learning activities (often referred to as continuous provision) will feature resources to support and develop children's interest in the book. Accordingly, the book corner would feature several copies of the text, as well as some non-fiction books about dinosaurs and butterflies, small world characters would support children to act out the story and retell the story and the writing area would obviously have a range of magic chalks! Other resources, such as a role play area, construction, mathematical resources and investigation areas would also be available, but some activities such as painting, junk modelling, sand and water play may be reserved for the afternoon session, depending on space and adult resources.

Sequence of learning

We have broken this sequence of learning into six sessions, but this can be shortened or lengthened depending on the extent to which children are involved and interested in the book. Small group sessions can be repeated on other days with other groups of children. It is important to remember that if your continuous provision is well planned and of high quality, children not working with an adult can be learning just as much, if not more, than those who are working in a focused group. If resources from previous days' lessons are added to the continuous provision (for example, sequencing pictures to retell the story), there are further opportunities for children to consolidate their learning. When an adult is available to support continuous provision, children will benefit from promotion of language development as well as Personal, Social and Emotional Development through sensitive facilitation of the activities in which the children are engaged.

Break time (15 minutes)

This is likely to be a completely new experience for Year 1 children and the rules and routines will need to be explained. It will be helpful if there are some quiet areas for children who find playtime with older children too boisterous.

Session 4 – Mathematics (45–60 minutes)

After a short whole-class introduction to a new concept, the teacher will work with a group of children. The rest of the children will select activities from a range of open-ended activities related to the learning objective, pitched to enable access and challenge for all children, within the continuous provision. Ideally, these activities should take place inside and outside the classroom but we recognise that staffing constraints may mean this is not possible.

What does this look like in practice?

We have seen teachers effectively plan a range of practical activities based around the objective for the session. For this purpose, we will use the example of Time. The short

Whole class/group	Activity	Link to Year 1 NC objectives
Lesson 1 – whole class; TA (if available) to support any children who cannot manage a whole-class session.	As an introduction to the text, the teacher would share the front cover of the book with the whole class and ask a range of questions such as; *What do you think is going to happen in this story? Why do you think that? What might be in the bag? How might this affect what happens in the story? Is this a friendly dinosaur? How do you know?* Children discuss their ideas verbally then use whiteboards or large paper to record their responses. These responses could be pictorial or written and completed individually or with a partner. Children can share ideas with the whole class or group and teachers can model correct sentence structure with high level vocabulary. The teacher will then share the story with the class, asking questions to promote thought and at the end, ask the class to summarise the story with her. At the end of this session children are free to access the continuous provision resources in the classroom; the adult's role is to engage with the children, talking with them and facilitating children's learning.	*Spoken language* - Listen and respond appropriately to adults and their peers. - Ask relevant questions to extend their understanding and knowledge. - Give well- structured descriptions, explanations and narratives including for expressing feelings. - Maintain attention and participate actively in collaborative conversations. - Use spoken language to develop understanding. - Speak audibly and fluently. *Reading* Develop pleasure in reading, motivation to read, vocabulary and understanding by: - Being encouraged to link what they hear to their own experiences. - Discussing word meanings. Linking new meanings to those already known. - Discussing the significance of the title and events. - Making inferences on the basis of what is being said and done.

(Continued)

Whole class/group	Activity	Link to Year 1 NC objectives
.		- Predicting what might happen on the basis of what has been read so far. - Participate in discussion about what is read to them. - Clearly explain their understanding of what is read to them. *Writing* Transcription: - Apply simple spelling rules. Composition: - Write sentences by saying out loud what they are going to write about. - Composing a sentence orally before writing it. - Sequencing sentences to form short narratives - Re-reading what they have written to check it makes sense.
Lesson 2 Small group activity adult- and child-initiated play-based learning	The teacher will retell the story to the class, then children will act out the story through role play and small world play, in small groups. Other children will want to play with construction, and other resources and that is absolutely fine – children absorbed in their own interests are learning. They may not be doing exactly what the adult has planned for them at that particular moment but the role of the adult is to assess what they can do and to try to build in opportunities within the continuous provision to address any gaps.	

Whole class/group	Activity	Link to Year 1 NC objectives
Lesson 3 Small group activity and child-initiated play	The focus for this session is to retell the story, putting the events in the correct chronological order. This could be done independently on large paper with felt tip pens by some children, or with an adult using picture prompts to sequence the story. As they are ordering the story, adults would encourage the children to talk about each part and introduce new vocabulary. The teacher would encourage children to think about different words they could use to connect events together (time related conjunctions) and model these to the children in sentences. Children could use large pieces of paper or whiteboards to write sentences in groups/pairs. Children not working with an adult would be free to access the continuous provision – they could complete the adult focussed small group activity at another time or on another day.	
Lesson 4 Whole class, adult-directed	The next session could be a practical lesson where the children find a bag of magic chalk in the classroom. The teacher could ask the children what types of things they would like to draw, and what they think might happen to their drawings. They can then take the children outside to draw things on the playground. In one of our schools, the teacher drew a person holding a small dog and asked the children to close their eyes. As if by magic, a member of staff suddenly appeared with her dog on a lead as if the drawing had come to life. This practical session really inspired and excited the children. Even if your school could not cope with bringing dogs on to the playground, there will be other things that, with a bit of forethought and planning, could magically come to life (a large bunch of flowers, a basket of fruit, a football could all be found hidden in a box or behind a shrub!).	

(Continued)

Whole class/group	Activity	Link to Year 1 NC objectives
Lesson 5 Whole class, small group activity and child-initiated play	This session focuses on descriptive language. Re-read the story or share photographs on the interactive whiteboard of the lesson that was taught outside in the previous session. Ask the children to describe how they felt when their drawings magically came to life, or how the children in the story felt when the dinosaur came to life. Explain to the children what an adjective is. In small groups, ask children to think of words to describe different parts of the text. Teachers can model up-levelling these words and create a word bank together. This can be displayed or printed into word mats for the children to use in independent writing. Other children can access the continuous provision independently; resources used in previous lessons are left out for independent access.	
Lesson 6 Whole class, small group or paired activity	The next lesson, which could well be spread over two days, will recap the previous sessions but have a written focus where the children retell the story. This does not mean all children sit at tables and chairs. Children can lie on their tummies on the carpet with whiteboards and pens, large sheets of paper can be put on tables with different coloured pens, chalks can be put outside, picture prompts can be spread across the tables for children who need a scaffold. Some children may retell the whole story using descriptive language, some may write simple sentences about each part of the story and some may label a picture. Children can work in small groups with an adult or in mixed-ability pairs to support one another and share ideas. You will know your children and it is important to be clear about your expectations of them. In addition to the objectives listed on the right, teachers will want to constantly reinforce the vocabulary, grammar and punctuation objectives. At the start of the year many children might only write a couple of sentences, but it is important to ensure they are remembering their capital letters, full stops and finger spaces. These key skills need to be embedded and some children are likely to need to be constantly reminded to use them. By the end of the year children will be writing for different purposes and the skills needed to do this will be taught through these sessions.	

whole-class session introduced children to how to tell time to the hour and half past the hour (a Year 1 National Curriculum expectation). The class teacher then took a group of children who were clearly struggling with this and together they made a clock face from a large hoop. The teacher was careful to model clearly how to place the numbers and then the hands in the correct position. A teaching assistant worked with another group sequencing months of the year in chronological order using correct mathematical language. Other children chose from a range of directed activities, including counting how many jumps they could complete in a minute and then independently recorded their results in a table (drawn in chalk on the playground) and compared the outcomes. Some children practised their fine motor skills, picking up small pompoms with tweezers and seeing how many they could drop in a container in one minute. Some chose to make watches and clocks in the creative area; others independently consolidated the work they had completed with the teaching assistant by making leaflets sequencing the months of the year. The classroom had an investigation table with a selection of clocks and time-pieces for children to explore. Children were free to access these activities just as they were used to doing in EYFS. All of these activities formed part of the wider continuous provision within the classroom. Although teachers sometimes decided to limit the number of activities available to children during the Mathematics session, it is important to note they were all practical with active hands-on learning. Worksheets are not allowed!

End of the morning (15 minutes)

A time to recap on the morning's learning and get ready for lunch.

Lunchtime (one hour)

If lunchtime arrangements are different from what children are used to in EYFS, they may need extra support and reassurance; it can be quite overwhelming for some children to enter a large noisy dining hall if they have been used to eating their lunch with just their year group. During lunchtime Year 1 staff set up the classroom ready for the afternoon activities; sometimes this means making more activities available, at other times it can be to refresh the activities that have been available in the morning so they are well organised, replenished and inviting.

Session 5 (15 minutes)

The time straight after lunch could be used as a time to practise fine or gross motor control skills, a music session or additional whole-class phonics session to focus on any sounds with which children might need extra support following on from the morning phonics sessions. Handwriting can be taught as a small group activity – some children will be ready to sit at a table and practise letter formation; others will still need lots of practice with fine and gross motor control. It is interesting to note that the National

Curriculum document recognises that one of the reasons children's writing in Year 1 generally develops at a slower pace than reading is because children need to "develop the physical skill needed for handwriting" (DfE, 2013, p. 19). Maria Robinson (2008) points out that children's wrist bones are not fully developed until about the age of six so it is important to ensure that activities aimed at improving handwriting are appropriate. Getting a class of five-to-six-year-olds to sit down at a table and all practise writing the letter "c", for example, is likely to result in fidgety, bored children. It would be far more beneficial for teachers to use their professional judgement to assess which children are ready for formal handwriting practice and which need support in further developing their fine and gross motor skills. Activities to develop fine motor control include using tweezers to pick up objects, using fine paintbrushes and threading or making patterns on small peg boards. Some children will benefit from activities to support gross motor control, including chalking letters on the playground, or taking part in practical sessions that involve music and movement. Other children may use whiteboards and pens to practise their letter formation.

Session 6 (90–120 minutes)

The bulk of the afternoon will be a continuous provision (free flow) session which will take place inside and outside of the classroom for at least four afternoons a week. What we mean by free flow is that a range of activities is set up both inside and outside and children are free to choose any activity that interests them. It is important that all adults working in a free flow setting understand the rationale and are committed to the provision to ensure it is successful. The fifth afternoon could be used for Physical Education or a discrete teaching of a specific subject such as Science. If children have access to continuous provision, which includes opportunities to develop gross and fine motor skills, as is the case in Reception, they will be able to cover comfortably the requirements of the National Curriculum for PE with one formal lesson a week. One of the schools in which we have carried out our research is fortunate to have a large shared space outside the three classrooms and they have been able to use this space to create a large workshop area with resources accessible for children to use independently and a spacious role play area that the whole year group can access. It is filled with resources, including things children can bring in from home and doors are left open so they can independently access the resources they want as and when they would like to, when working at the creative area (Figures 4.2 and 4.3).

Putting ideas into practice 65

Figure 4.2 Creative workshop shared area

Figure 4.3 Storing resources shared area

School leaders will need to make sure there is a curriculum map in place for the term and a system for ensuring teachers can track coverage of foundation subjects. Topics should be chosen to engage and interest children with activities within the continuous provision carefully planned to achieve the desired outcome.

Adult- and child-initiated activities

It might be helpful here to describe how we distinguish between the different types of provision. Adult-directed activities are those planned by an adult with a clear learning outcome in mind. Adult-initiated play-based activities are set up by an adult as part of the continuous provision; they may or may not have a specific learning outcome, but will always be linked to the core text or theme. Child-initiated activities are those activities instigated and developed by children. It is key that there is a balance between activities that have a planned outcome and also more open-ended activities which do not necessarily have a clear learning intention but which nevertheless have an inbuilt challenge. For example, if children were learning about minibeasts, an investigative table could be provided with real and model insects, pieces of wood, leaves, bark, magnifying glasses, microscopes, non-fiction books, photographs, blank charts and leaflets. This would be adult-initiated. The adult input could be questions such as; Are butterflies and moths or bees and wasps the same? Do spiders fly? Children might then take their own learning in a different direction perhaps by designing and making a super bug in the creative modelling area, by exploring colours and making patterns, using a computer to make a leaflet about similarities and differences, making and recording some bug music or a bug dance – the list goes on and on! It is often in these activities where children have decided to take their learning on in a direction that they have decided that we see the highest levels of engagement and concentration. One girl was so fascinated by the colours in a dragonfly's wing she decided to create patterns using blue and green paints; this had not been planned by the teacher and wasn't specifically extending her knowledge of minibeasts, but was a highly worthwhile activity in which she was able to explore, create and mix different shades of colours.

Free flow

Karen, a Year 1 teacher in one of our schools, states "to get free flow right, you have to put a lot of energy and creativity into it. It is important to invigorate and accommodate the needs of all children." She points out that "free flow is non-directive so it is important for the staff in Year 1 to have the ability to challenge children throughout the activities".

Our free flow activities are based around the core text or topic, but, as described above, these are starting points and children are free to take their learning on in different directions. Activities include the resources available in the morning session with some additional activities set up at lunchtime. Staff are careful to note which activities interest the children and are quick to change things if they notice that a particular activity is not accessed. Children will have access to a role play area, book corner, small world, workshop area, construction, messy play and opportunities for physical development and activities to promote creativity. There should be opportunities to develop writing skills in all activities. Free flow sessions mean children can work individually, or in mixed-ability pairs or groups supporting each other.

An example of a medium-term plan for a topic based around the traditional tale of *The Three Little Pigs* is provided in Figure 4.4.

What does this look like in practice?

The afternoon starts with a whole-class carpet session at the beginning of the afternoon, when a new theme or skill is introduced. Children are then free to access the independent learning activities with one group remaining with the teacher. This session usually focuses on the development of writing skills within a cross-curricular context, although at least once a week there is a focus on reading. We have found this to be a very effective strategy in the first two terms, with the teacher providing intensive support for children of all abilities, as it allows for instant feedback. Once children have completed their writing, they are free to access the continuous provision and the teacher will usually then take another group or perhaps support children in their free flow activities; the long, uninterrupted session comfortably provides enough time for at least two groups to benefit from the teacher's focus on their writing progress.

We have found short, intensive writing sessions with small groups of children in these afternoon sessions during the first few months in Year 1 to be vital in securing progress in writing. Figures 4.5 and 4.6 show the development in one boy's writing from the beginning of October in Year 1 to six months later at the end of March.

Whilst one group is working with the teacher, the teaching assistant will support the continuous provision and may work with other groups to address any misconceptions from the morning session or, once the children are all engaged, may lead an activity based on the theme. Many of the independent learning activities will be linked to the topic and core text and children can continue to investigate and explore the mathematical activities from the morning. Children should be able to independently work at art and design technology activities and if the outdoor learning area is available a range of activities can be set up there. There should be writing opportunities available at all activities, which children are encouraged to use.

As the overall theme is "Dinosaurs", we will continue to provide a range of activities which fit in with both this theme and the core text. The creative workshop will be available in the afternoon for children to explore; they may want to make papier-mâché dinosaur eggs, or a large dinosaur made from junk modelling. Others will want to paint pictures or make 3D dinosaur lands. However, as we have just read the story of *Chalk*, others will want to make a model which they can then pretend comes to life. Teachers

Writing Opportunities

Use outlines of a pig and wolf to write descriptive words in to describe the characters, children to then write descriptive sentences

Re-tell the story by writing own book –have blank books readily available for the children to use with pink front covers – children can us felt tip pens, colouring pencils and pencils. They can illustrate this themselves. Children to use adjectives to describe. They can design their own front cover

English objective -Sequencing sentences to form short narratives re-reading what they have written to check that it makes sense

Art and DT

Children to create the three houses using different materials –what will you use to fix them together? Ensure there are a range of resources available or the children to access independently.
Colour mixing

Art and Design objective -to use a range of materials creatively to design and make products

to develop a wide range of art and design techniques in using colour, pattern, texture, line, shape, form and space

ICT

Create a beebot mat with different parts of the story – children to programme the beebot to move to a certain part of the mat, when it reaches that part children to describe what happens
Computing objective - recognise common uses of information technology beyond school

Topic: Traditional Tales

Core Text: The three little pigs

Free flow activities

Communication and Language/ role play

Tuff spots with small world play for children to re-tell the story – can you create your own ending? Can you use resources to create the setting of the story?
Children to create their own masks to re tell the story

Spoken language objective -participate in discussions, presentations, performances, role play

Outside area

Children to build the three little pigs houses – create a large construction area where children can design the houses, have real bricks, sticks and straw, large boxes and crates. Give children a variety of materials to choose from and work out which would be stronger to use so if the wolf blows it down will it last?
Science objective - identify and name a variety of everyday materials, including wood, plastic, glass, metal, water, and rock

describe the simple physical properties of a variety of everyday materials

Geometry properties of shapes -recognise and name common 2-D and 3-D shapes, including: 2-D shapes [for example, rectangles (including squares), circles and triangles], 3-D shapes [for example, cuboids (including cubes), pyramids and spheres].

Measurement objective - Pupils should compare, describe and solve practical problems for: lengths and heights [for example, long/short, longer/shorter, tall/short, double/half]

Large stage for role play for children to re – tell the story

Writing tool kits for children to write the story

Music

Have a range of musical instruments available or the children to use to re-tell the story through role play –what instrument will you use to show the wolf is coming?
Children to chant 'I am going to huff, and puff and blow your house down'

Music objective - use their voices expressively and creatively by singing songs and speaking chants and rhymes

play tuned and untuned instruments musically

All of these activities allow children to work together collaboratively and creatively. Social skills are developed through this provision and It also means that children have the opportunity to;

- *use spoken language to develop understanding through speculating, hypothesising, imagining and exploring ideas*
- *speak audibly and fluently with an increasing command of Standard English*
- *listen and respond appropriately to adults and their peers*
- *ask relevant questions to extend their understanding and knowledge*
- *use relevant strategies to build their vocabulary*
- *articulate and justify answers, arguments and opinions*

These are Spoken Language objectives from the National Curriculum English programme of study.

Figure 4.4 Medium-term plan: *The Three Little Pigs*

Putting ideas into practice 69

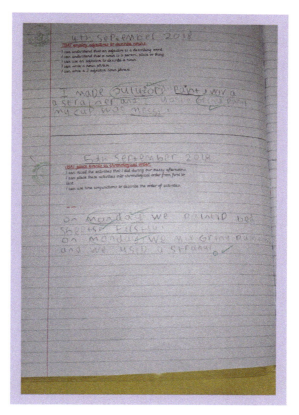

Figure 4.5 Boy's writing – September

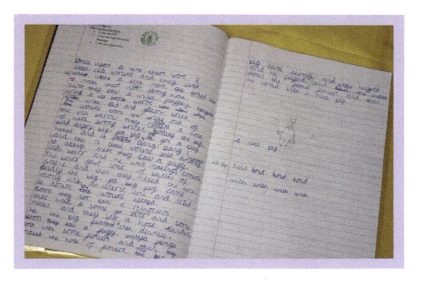

Figure 4.6 Boy's writing – March

may leave the magic bag of chalk in the outside area for children to use and set up a writing area with resources from the morning session for children to access and write independently. Resources are open-ended and independently accessed and children are free to choose how or if they will use this area. An adult-led messy play activity could be to make dinosaur footprints which can be used for ordering numbers, and counting in twos. Other adult-initiated activities could be hidden dinosaur vocabulary in the sand for children to identify and squirting water pistols at common exception words displayed on the wall outside and using these words to form sentences. It is important to plan activities that allow children to work together and provide resources for children to access themselves with no templates. Giving children a range of resources means they can choose what they would like to use and take ownership of their own learning. Once all children have settled to an activity, the teacher is then free to work with a group of children and support them to secure any gaps they may have, giving instant feedback.

The role of the adult in free flow

The role of the adult is to facilitate learning, but how do we go about this? Firstly, it is important that there is an adult to facilitate free flow; if children are left to their own devices, they may feel their play is not valued and the quality of that play can quickly degenerate. So, although one adult may be working with a group it is important that there is another adult to support and facilitate free flow across the continuous provision. Support and training for adults is vital as being able to judge when to intervene to move learning on is not easy. We recommend our staff read Julie Fisher's book *Interacting or Interfering? Improving Interactions in the Early Years* (Fisher, 2016) One of our biggest challenges was to ensure adults encourage children to be independent and to try to solve problems themselves. It is a very human response to try to do things for children, especially if we see they are struggling. However, it is really important to allow children time to work things out for themselves and to resist the temptation to launch ourselves in to "help". We have given our less experienced teachers and teaching assistants a range of open-ended questions which are designed to act as prompts for children to discuss their learning in depth. These prompts include:

We have found that "I wonder whether …" is a particularly useful starting point to provide a suggestion rather than saying "Why don't you?"

Putting ideas into practice 71

72 Putting ideas into practice

The other important role for the adult is to feedback to the teacher any significant information that they may have noticed during the day.

Some teachers may ask where can interventions fit in. If continuous provision is planned effectively, there will be little need for interventions as the activities can be planned to address any gaps. However, we recognise that some children will have specific targets from personalised plans and adults can support children to achieve these through carefully planned individual tasks. These can take place throughout the free flow session and activities can be planned to ensure targets from personalised plans can be met.

How does this session develop throughout the year?

As the year progresses, the balance of teacher-led and child-led activities will change and towards the end of the year there may well be at least two afternoons given over to discrete subjects. The teacher-led reading and writing groups will also change, with the majority of children expected to use their developing writing skills to work more independently and without the intensive adult support which was in place at the beginning of the year. Some exemplar timetables are provided in the Appendix to Chapter 1.

Session 7 class story time (15–20 minutes)

The end of the day is when the class comes together for a story. It is really important for children to be exposed to a variety of texts. As the children will have a core text to focus on as part of their English session, teachers can use this time to read different stories that may or may not relate to their topic. It is important that Year 1 pupils have a dedicated story time every day as well as experiencing reading at other times of the day.

End of the day

This again should be a relaxed time for children as well as the teacher; it should provide opportunities for teachers and children to review the day's learning, to celebrate successes and to give parents positive messages about their children's achievements.

Planning

One of the biggest differences between teaching in EYFS and Year 1 is the move from a holistic curriculum based on areas of learning to a subject-based curriculum. Teachers often worry how they can be sure they are covering the Year 1 programme of study in the National Curriculum in a play-based provision, so children can demonstrate they have met the end of year expectations.

Some schools list the statutory requirements for each of the subjects and record when they have been taught as part of a topic or arising from a core text. For example, traditional tales such as *Little Red Riding Hood* or *The Gingerbread Man* could spark a discussion about carnivores, herbivores and omnivores – as part of the continuous provision teachers could then set up an activity where children sort animals into the various groups. *The Three Little Pigs* lends itself beautifully to an investigation of materials and their properties. Studying these concepts as part of an overall theme gives meaning to the learning; building houses out of different materials, testing them for strength over the course of a week or so in continuous provision, is likely to lead to much deeper embedded learning than a lesson asking children to describe materials and their properties out of context and to record that information in an exercise book. A well-planned investigation table such as the ones in Figures 4.7–4.10 can give children opportunities to cover all the statutory requirements of working scientifically:

> *During Years 1 and 2, pupils should be taught to use the following practical scientific methods, processes and skills through the teaching of the programme of study content:*
>
> - *asking simple questions and recognising that they can be answered in different ways*
> - *observing closely, using simple equipment*
> - *performing simple tests*
> - *identifying and classifying using their observations and ideas to suggest answers to questions, gathering and recording data to help in answering questions.*
>
> (DfE, 2013)

Figure 4.7 Science investigation area

Putting ideas into practice 75

Figure 4.8 Science investigation area

Figure 4.9 Science investigation area

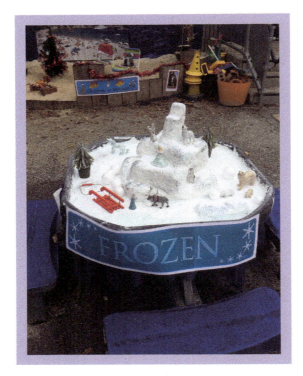

Figure 4.10 Science investigation area

Karen at Istead Rise Primary School devised a long-term plan where she matched the objectives set out in the statutory requirements and, having determined what interested the children in that particular cohort, worked out where the objectives fitted best over the year. She was able to use this plan to check she had included all the objectives set out in the statutory requirements of the Year 1 National Curriculum programmes of study. From this, she drew up some medium-term plans – examples of which are given in Figures 4.11 and 4.12 to this chapter.

Assessment

When children reach the end of their time in the Early Years Foundation Stage, their profile results mean schools have a wealth of information about them across a whole range of domains. In fact, it could be argued that at no point in their future education is so much information available; not just about their literacy and numeracy skills, but also with regard to their attitudes to learning, their Personal, Social, Emotional and Physical Development and their communication and language skills as well as strengths and areas for development in all the other areas of learning.

In order to be able to seamlessly plan from children's starting points, it is really important that Year 1 teachers and senior leaders fully understand this range of information.

Year 1	Term 2, (7 weeks)
Topic	**Superheroes**
Foundation Subject Focus	Science , History
Core texts	Supertato Traction man is here Eliot Midnight , Superhero Superdaisy Newspaper boy and origami girl
English – writing genres	Write a newspaper report (Superhero report) Character description Narrative superhero story
Spelling, Punctuation and Grammar	Spelling patterns - or, air, ir, ou , oy, ea,oi Regular past tense Suffix "ing, est, ed, er" Common exception words Days of the week Simple monosyllabic words Punctuation – capital letters at beginning of sentence, proper noun and personal pronoun "I". Full stops , exclamation marks Grammar: adjectives , nouns, time adverbials, conjunctions
Vocabulary (Wow words)	Superlative, awe inspiring extraordinary, colossal, incredible, superhuman
Mathematics	Number: place value, • count to and across 100, forwards and backwards, beginning with 0 or 1, or from any given number • given a number, identify one more and one less Number - addition, subtraction Geometry - Recognise and name common 2-D and 3-D shapes
Science	Materials • distinguish between an object and the material from which it is made. • identify and name a variety of everyday materials, including wood, plastic, glass, metal, water, and rock • describe the simple physical properties of a variety of everyday materials • compare and group together a variety of everyday materials on the basis of their simple physical properties. Identify and compare the suitability of a variety of everyday materials for specific purposes including wood, metal, plastic, glass, brick, rock, paper. Senses – continuous provision – choose a supersense for your superhero – draw, label and write.
History	Changes within living memory. Where appropriate, these should be used to reveal aspects of change in national life. Significant historical events, people and places in their own locality. (local heroes)

Figure 4.11 Medium-term plan: Superheroes

Year 1	Term 5 (6 weeks)
Topic	**Pirates**
Foundation Subject Focus	Geography, History , DT
Core texts	Peter Pan The Owl and the Pussycat The Night Pirates Pocahontas Pirates love underpants
English – writing genres	Fiction - description – desert island setting Non-fiction – instructions – how to dress like a pirate Fiction, letter in a bottle Fiction, narrative, pirate story Class book – pirate jokes
Spelling, Punctuation and Grammar	Spelling patterns -ire, ear, ure, ie, au Prefix "un" Punctuation - Capital letters, full stops, exclamation marks, question marks Grammar : adjectives, nouns, noun phrases, time adverbials, conjunctions first person
Vocabulary (Wow words)	Gluttonous, cunning, marooned, ferocious , lawless, notorious, nautical, plunder, swagger
Mathematics	Number: place value <ul><li>count, read and write numbers to 100 in numerals; count in multiples of twos, fives and tens</li><li>identify and represent numbers using objects and pictorial representations including the number line, and use the language of: equal to, more than, less than (fewer), most, least</li></ul>Measurement, money - recognise and know the value of different denominations of coins and notes
Science	Seasons <ul><li>observe changes across the four seasons</li><li>observe and describe weather associated with the seasons and how day length varies.</li></ul>Continuous Provision (investigation table) Working Scientifically <ul><li>asking simple questions and recognising that they can be answered in different ways</li><li>observing closely, using simple equipment</li><li>performing simple tests</li><li>identifying and classifying</li><li>using their observations and ideas to suggest answers to questions</li><li>gathering and recording data to help in answering questions.</li></ul>
History	Understand the lives of significant individuals in the past who have contributed to national and international achievements, comparing aspects of life in different periods. (Christopher Columbus and Neil Armstrong – travellers -would Christopher Columbus have encountered pirates? Might there be pirates in space in the future?)

Geography	Geographical skills and fieldwork Use simple compass directions (North, South, East and West) and locational and directional language [for example, near and far; left and right], to describe the location of features and routes on a map. (Follow a pre drawn map first then children to design their own maps and find the buried treasure) Use aerial photographs and plan perspectives to recognise landmarks and basic human and physical features; devise a simple map; and use and construct basic symbols in a key Use world maps, atlases and globes to identify the United Kingdom and its countries, as well as the countries, continents and oceans studied at this key stage (where did the pirates travel?)
Design and technology	Evaluate explore and evaluate a range of existing products Design design purposeful, functional, appealing products for themselves and other users based on design criteria (design a pirate ship) Make select from and use a range of tools and equipment to perform practical tasks [for example, cutting, shaping, joining and finishing] evaluate their ideas and products against design criteria (pirate ship –does it float?)

Figure 4.12 Medium-term plan: Pirates

Too often in the past we have seen Year 1 teachers, with the best of intentions, grouping children according to whether they have achieved a GLD, were working towards or had exceeded the goals. Teachers need to understand that even when children have not yet met the criteria for GLD, they could well have literacy and numeracy skills which are at the expected standards for their age.

Much of the assessment information in the EYFS is gained from observing children whilst they are absorbed in their play and this is a skill that Year 1 teachers will find very useful. If, for example, simple addition skills are taught in an active, playful way such as children generating their own sums by throwing beanbags into numbered hoops and recording the results in chalk on the playground, teachers will immediately be able to see who has mastered the skill and who needs further support. In addition, teachers will also gather information on children's confidence and fluency with number – how quickly they were able to calculate the sums, give instant feedback to the group on the accuracy of recording the numbers as well as observe physical and social development such as turn-taking. As well as being much more interesting – and fun – for children than completing a worksheet or recording sums in an exercise book, a teacher observing that activity will have much more detailed information than would be possible from setting a whole class a task of completing a set of sums and marking a set of books. Chapter 6 describes the experience of a teacher new to Year 1 who was at first unsure about how best to implement a play-based approach, but who confirmed she knew her children much better than any other class she had ever taken through taking time to observe them and focussing as much as possible on small group rather than whole-class teaching. One of the factors we noted when commenting on the rapid progress children were making in our afternoon small group writing sessions, was that teachers were able to give instant feedback. These sessions enabled teachers to know exactly where children's strengths and areas for development lay and this was a key factor in children's rapid progress in writing. In time, this led to children developing their own self-assessment skills and looking through their work and attempting to "make it better" by including more "wow" words, adjectives or different sentence openings.

Schools are likely to have developed their own summative assessment systems which will be informed by pupil progress meetings, as well as regular discussions amongst teachers arising from day-to-day formative assessment, as described above. Annotated photographs are helpful in providing a record of children's achievements and these can also contribute towards class books as a record and celebration of termly topics. As described above, medium-term plans can be drawn up from a long-term plan which matches the objectives set out in the National Curriculum with themes that reflect children's interests.

Summary

When talking to Year 1 teachers who have followed this timetable, they have recognised children's deep level of engagement, especially in free flow activities. When changing from formal teaching to this way, the biggest challenge for teachers was allowing children to lead their learning. It was a real shock for some teachers to realise that children following their interests during free flow activities were often far livelier, more focussed and deeply engaged in cross-curricular learning than they would ever have been in a more formal lesson style. However, it is important to ensure activities have a suitable in-built level of challenge and teachers do need to develop the confidence to change their planning if things are not working. Teachers commented that they were very pleased at the way children continued to build upon the personal, social and emotional skills that they had demonstrated in the EYFS classes and collaborative learning was a strong feature of much of the curriculum. They found that having small focus groups during free flow meant they were able to accurately assess children's understanding and immediately address misconceptions and identify next steps. Well-planned free flow activities meant that children were able to consolidate and apply their learning. Disadvantaged pupils, in particular, really benefit from a curriculum closely tailored to their interests.

It is important that schools continue to promote spiritual, moral, social and cultural development through a range of enrichment activities. Memorable occasions that enable children to experience awe and wonder and a fascination with the world will enhance their learning across a wide range of curriculum subjects.

Staff may need to adapt the way they organise their classroom – not all Year 1 classrooms will have direct access to an outside area, so schools may need to review the location of Year 1 classrooms for future years. In order to achieve best outcomes for children, staffing ratios may also need to be reviewed. For example, ideally each class in a two-form entry school will need a teacher and a full-time teaching assistant. However, we recognise that with squeezed budgets in schools this may not be possible and we have seen a highly effective, playful approach to learning in place in schools where there is a teaching assistant in each Year 1 class, in addition to the class teacher, only in the morning.

REFLECTION

■ What will be the biggest challenge for teachers in changing practice from a formal to a play-based curriculum?

■ How different do you think the provision in Year 1 should be at the beginning and the end of the year?

References

Department for Education (DfE) (2013) *The National Curriculum in England*, reference DfE-00177-2013. London: DfE.

Fisher, J. (2016) *Interacting or Interfering? Improving Interactions in the Early Years*. Maidenhead: Open University Press.

Robinson, M. (2008) *Child Development from Birth to Eight*. Maidenhead: Open University Press.

Standards and Testing Agency (2018) *The Early Years Foundation Stage Handbook*, reference STA/19/8311/e. London: STA.

Thomson, W. (2010) *Chalk*. Singapore: Marshall Cavendish.

5 Barriers to implementation

Our evidence as described in Chapters 3 and 4 has clearly shown that children in Year 1 benefit from a curriculum which is based around their interests and is delivered in a way which puts learning in a meaningful context. So why is this approach still the exception rather than the rule?

External pressures

Ofsted

Many schools broadly welcomed HMCI's announcements (December 2018) which set out Ofsted's intention to focus more on the curriculum and less on outcomes in the 2019 framework. (Ofsted 2019).

However, the publication in November 2017 of the document *Bold Beginnings: the reception curriculum in a sample of good and outstanding primary schools* (Ofsted 2017) caused some confusion in schools. There was an implicit message in this report that the Reception year should prepare children for the demands of the Year 1 curriculum with a clear underlying agenda of downward pressure from KS1 to narrow the Early Years curriculum. The report's first recommendation that "the teaching of reading is the core purpose of the reception year" is a very different standpoint from the widely accepted view that the Early Years Foundation Stage (EYFS) provides a distinct curriculum and pedagogy that supports what is known about children's early learning and development. We completely endorse the response of TACTYC in their publication *"Bald Beginnings!"* (TACTYC 2017) that "the early years foundation stage curriculum should focus on the overwhelming evidence that young children aged four- and five-years need a broad-based curriculum that encourages foundational learning and development across all domains, but with particular emphasis on physical, social and emotional, and language and communication development." TACTYC goes on to quote Kangas et al. (2015):

"The main goal of early years education should be the development of executive functions that are strongly indicative of school success" (TACTYC 2017).

TACTYC's first recommendation in response to their critique of *Bold Beginnings* is that "Rather than defining the EYFS as preparation for Year 1, the content of the national curriculum for Year 1 should be reviewed, so that there is greater alignment between the necessarily broad-based EYFS/EYFSP and the expectations for Year 1." Whilst fully endorsing this statement, our view is that there is currently scope to promote greater alignment between the end of EYFS and the end of year expectations for Year 1 by focussing less on what is taught, but more on how young children engage with the learning process.

In her book *Moving on to Key Stage 1 – improving transition from the Early Years Foundation Stage*, Julie Fisher succinctly states that "Until there is recognition that *how* we teach children has every bit as much impact on outcomes and standards as *what* children are taught, then children's progress will continue to plateau. All teachers need to understand how their children learn best and then have the professional autonomy to introduce that practice into their classrooms" (Fisher 2010). Our evidence shows that by planning work around a high-quality core text, it is possible to fully meet the end of year expectations for Year 1 in all subjects in a way that is fun and meaningful for children. Our approach recognises that in providing opportunities for children to choose how and where to record their work and to plan activities based on children's interests that meet the Year 1 objectives results in competent, confident learners. We know from our observations that many children, especially boys and younger children, do not thrive sitting indoors writing at a table for any length of time.

In recent years, Ofsted have carried out three phases of research into the school curriculum and in her commentary on phase 3 of this research, published 11 December 2018, Amanda Spielman, HMCI, noted:

> We found that many schools were teaching to the test and teaching a narrowed curriculum in pursuit of league table outcomes, rather than thinking about the careful sequencing of a broad range of knowledge and skills. This was disappointing but unsurprising. We have accepted that inspection itself is in part to blame. It has played too great a role in intensifying performance data rather than complementing it.
>
> (Spielman 2018)

Statutory assessments

However, in spite of this welcome admission that Ofsted itself is partly to blame for a focus on data, there is still a huge culture of testing for children who are required to take a number of statutory assessments throughout their time in English primary schools. At the time of writing, as well as the end of KS2 SATs, profile assessments currently take place at the end of EYFS and there is a phonic screening check at the end of Year 1. Formal tests in English and Mathematics inform statutory teacher assessment at the end of Year 2, although these end of KS1 assessments are due to be phased out by 2023. In addition, the Year 4 times table tests have been implemented and plans to introduce a baseline assessment for children starting school in 2020 are well advanced. These on-entry baseline tests are not intended as a formative measure to help teachers identify children's achievements and plan next steps, but are to be used purely as an accountability measure for schools. Children's early literacy and numeracy skills are to be compared with their attainment at the end of Year 6 and used as a progress indicator for the school. In spite of significant objections from school leaders and parents who are opposed to the introduction of this baseline assessment, because of concerns about the validity of the data and the departure from what is widely regarded as good Early Years practice (Bradbury A. and Roberts-Holmes G. 2016) and (More than a Score 2018 *Baseline assessment: Why it doesn't add up*) at the time of writing, it appears to be going ahead.

Leadership

Results from each of these statutory assessments are reported in each schools' "dashboard" where the performance of whole cohorts and groups is compared with all schools nationally. This inevitably creates pressure on governors, headteachers and school leaders to improve results year on year. These pressures lead many schools into adopting a more formal approach to learning. There are several reasons for this; many school leaders have little direct experience of teaching the youngest children and they often see a didactic approach to teaching as being the most effective in securing results. Comments and recommendations in *Bold Beginnings* (Ofsted 2017) include "They used pencils and exercise books, while children sat at tables, to support good, controlled letter formation"; "The headteachers knew which aspects of learning needed to be taught directly and which could be learned through play" and schools should "Devote sufficient time each day to the direct teaching of reading, writing and mathematics." These comments give a clear (though, in the authors' view, erroneous) message that children in Reception should be moving to a more formal way of learning ready for Year 1, with the implicit message that formal learning will be the norm in Year 1. It is unsurprising that many school leaders feel under pressure to move away from a child-centred, play-based approach to a more traditional model of teaching. Some research indicates there may be some evidence of short-term gains with a more formal approach; however, didactic approaches appear to undermine young children's motivation in, and enjoyment of, school and often have negative implications for long-term achievement. (Phillips and Stipek 1993). In the schools we have visited where there has been a smooth transition into Year 1 with a continuation of a play-based approach, school leaders have been supportive to teachers and confident that this is the right way to develop teaching and learning in Year 1 and beyond.

We visited a number of schools in the course of our research which frequently host visits from other schools because of their reputation in providing high-quality provision in both Reception and Year 1. Rockmount Primary School in Croydon and Pickhurst Infant Academy in Bromley are two schools already mentioned. The single universal message from each of these schools was that it was essential for headteachers to accompany staff when visiting schools to observe high-quality provision if there was a genuine desire to effect change in practice. Unless headteachers and senior leaders are able to understand and believe in the philosophy that young children learn best when the way curriculum is delivered is geared to their interests and developmental stages, then the impact of teachers visiting to see that provision will be limited.

Aside from the move to subject-based learning, there is certainly no expectation from the National Curriculum that there should be a change of approach as children move to Year 1 – in fact, just the opposite. The National Curriculum document (DfE 2013) specifically states that "schools are free to choose how they organise their school day" and that "during Year 1, teachers should build on work from the Early Years Foundation Stage." It refers to a "balanced and broadly-based curriculum" which "prepares pupils at the school for the opportunities, responsibilities and experiences of later life." Certainly, the authors have never understood why the life skills of independence, negotiation and decision-making which are such a feature of EYFS education should suddenly stop when children start Year 1 – yet how often have we walked into classrooms where pencils are set out in pots on tables, exercise books are handed out and children have little or no say in how, when or where they record their work.

Lack of understanding of how play supports children's learning and development

In one of the schools we visited, teachers and teaching assistants were genuinely worried that by continuing to let children "play" rather than work, we were holding them back. This lack of understanding about how play underpins learning for young children and is the vehicle through which they are able to make sense of their world is not uncommon in primary schools and Year 1 teachers may need some support in understanding the difference between child-initiated and adult-initiated play.

We were able to partially address this concern at this particular school by getting an EYFS teacher to talk through some of the activities he had set up and explain what the children had learned in a range of areas. There was also confusion in understanding the terminology of "continuous provision." Some teachers in Year 1 thought that meant we adopt a completely child-initiated approach, where children can access whatever resources they want as and when they want; whilst this is a perfectly legitimate approach and common in many pre-school and Early Years settings, we have developed a different methodology in our schools in Year 1. Teachers set up a number of areas linked to the theme or topic that children are learning about which can be accessed independently; these include construction, role play, sand, water and messy play, a creative area and an investigation table. Some activities will be entirely open-ended (child-initiated) with no intended learning outcome; for example, a workshop area with different sized boxes, tubes, scissors, measuring tapes, items for sticking and gluing, feathers, paints and so on. These resources need to be well organised and accessible and children need to learn how to use them, but the outcomes are not predetermined by an adult. It is often in these types of activities that children demonstrate the highest levels of involvement and concentration. Other activities (adult-initiated) will have a learning outcome attached. As children are learning new skills or specific concepts, these play-based activities can be planned and developed to address gaps in children's learning. For example, children in Year 1 learn about fractions and are expected to be able to find halves and quarters of shapes and quantities. Following clear modelling of how to halve and quarter shapes most children are reasonably quick to understand the concept of a half and a quarter and are able to explain and demonstrate that halving or quartering a shape means splitting it into two or four equal parts. However, being able to find a half or a quarter of a quantity of objects is more difficult for some. There are many ways to approach this in a playful manner – working out how many are left after the fraction giant has gobbled up half, a quarter or a third of the cakes; providing a bag of bricks (containing sixteen, twenty, twenty-four or more bricks) asking two children to make a model, then using half or a quarter of the bricks to make two or four smaller models. These are just two examples of how teachers have devised an effective, playful way of reinforcing a fairly abstract concept. As an extension, children might adapt a recipe to cater for smaller quantities – a useful skill in daily life for adults. An easy way to introduce this is to change the quantity of oats in porridge for the three bears; starting with 100 grams of oats for Daddy bear, then halving the quantity of oats for Mummy bear and halving again for Baby bear.

Standards

A lack of understanding of how play supports children's learning and development often leads to a concern about standards and how independent learning activities can support the development of skills.

Although one of the barriers to implementing a play-based approach in Year 1 is school leaders' perceptions that standards will be adversely affected, our own research indicates that there is no evidence that this is the case. In fact, the reverse is true. By teaching writing in small groups children made exceptional progress from their starting points, as is illustrated in Figures 5.1 and 5.2. The first piece was by a child who had been assessed as working at the expected level by the end of the Reception year. By March, she was writing independently and at length – in ink (how often do we decide that five- and six-year-olds should not have access to pens!)

88 Barriers to implementation

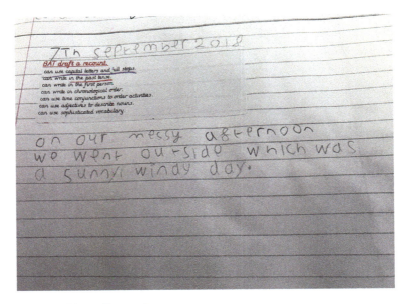

Figure 5.1 Girl's writing – September

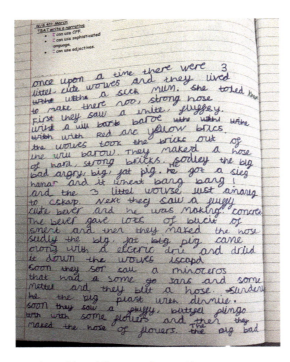

Figure 5.2 Improvement in writing skills over six months

CASE STUDY

Although it is fairly easy to assess progress in writing and Mathematics it is sometimes more difficult to assess progress in skills which are developed through independent learning activities. At Rockmount Primary School in Croydon, staff in Nursery, Reception and Year 1 have worked together to ensure skills across all areas are identified and that expectations of standards across the different year groups are clear. One member of staff has been given the responsibility to support teachers and additional adults to ensure there is an appropriate level of challenge across the continuous provision and to identify progression in skills. Staff in the three year groups agreed to focus on one specific area at a time, for example role play or sand or the workshop area. They visited each other's classrooms to see what activities were provided and to identify how learning was different in different year groups.

They agreed that as well as developing social skills, small world play is really important in a number of curriculum areas, including developing children's language and communication skills, Mathematics, Science and Geography. By focussing on one area of the continuous provision at a time they were able to draw up detailed guidance of the knowledge, skills and concepts children would tackle, the attitudes to learning that would be developed, the resources needed and their organisation, the learning outcomes (which were drawn from both the EYFS framework and the National Curriculum), what the children would be doing and how the adults could support the activity. These were then printed out as prompts for any adults who might be passing by that activity. An example of a Year 1 prompt sheet for small world activities is provided below (Figure 5.3) and a photograph of a small world activity with prompts alongside is shown in Chapter 3, Figure 3.8.

By concentrating on one area at a time for the continuous provision, the task of identifying the progression of skills across the three year groups and designing the prompt sheets was manageable. Teachers noted that in the nursery classes, children were playing with dinosaurs and using malleable materials to make their own dinosaurs and adding to the habitat. In the Reception classes, children's reading skills were being developed by the presence of relevant vocabulary, whilst in Year 1 children were encouraged to act out stories using the resources available and to record their conversations using the writing materials which were to hand. Prompts for adults were available at each area which identified the knowledge and skills children could be learning, what the teachers were expecting and the sorts of questions adults could ask.

Staff discussed the differences in provision in the three year groups and agreed to act as critical friends to each other. For readers who might find this notion of acting as a critical friend to a colleague slightly unnerving, it might be helpful to explain that senior leaders at Rockmount have developed a highly collaborative, inclusive approach to school improvement.

> *Several years ago, they recognised that formal monitoring with regular lesson observations was not improving practice; in fact, it was making teachers stressed and concerned about their "performance" on the day. Over recent years, they have set up a programme of informal learning walks, peer assessment and team teaching. Senior leaders work with teachers in the classroom, identifying strengths and modelling different ways of working. This approach has helped teachers to reflect on their practice and given them the confidence to learn from each other. The culture of whole-school accountability, where every member of staff is considered responsible for nurturing children's talents and potential and where staff are well supported by senior leaders to maintain the very highest expectations of what children can achieve, has resulted in a school where staff enjoy working together in order to further improve their own pedagogy.*

Mixed-ability grouping

In all the schools we visited where Year 1 was organised around children's interests, teachers were clear that splitting children into ability groups, still a very common practice in many schools even for Year 1 children, was not effective. They recognised children made better progress when working in mixed-ability groups or in pairs. This is not to say that children with specific needs should not receive individual support targeted to their requirements but, as Shirley Clarke stated: "When children are grouped by ability, expectations placed upon them tend to be fixed and children's achievement is matched to those expectations" (2014). There is little doubt that most children who are always on a "lower ability table" are unlikely to believe they can succeed as well as others in the class. The Sutton Trust (2011), quoted in Clarke (2014), makes the point that "The evidence is consistent that though there may be some benefits for higher attaining pupils in some circumstances, these are outweighed by the negative attitudes on middle and low performing learners." Some teachers think that young children are unaware they have been put into specific ability groups but recent research carried out by Bradbury and Roberts-Holmes (Bradbury and Roberts-Holmes 2017) for the National Education Union found this was not the case. In their findings published in *Grouping in Early Years and Key Stage 1 – a necessary evil?*, they quote Parsons and Hallam (2014) and Scherer (2016). Parsons and Hallam noted that "grouping does not improve attainment overall and that children are aware of and affected by the hierarchies imposed by grouping. They also quote one child, aged six, from Scherer's study who said, 'I am not clever, they are cleverer than us'" (Scherer 2016).

Barriers to implementation 91

Area of Provision: Small World	
Skills: • Sharing • Turn-taking • Setting a scene • Imagining • Describing • Explaining • Naming people and equipment • Making decisions	**Attitudes:** • Confidence • Co-operation • Sharing ideas • Interest/curiosity • Independence • Motivation to solve problems

Knowledge and Concepts:

- Play collaboratively and share resources
- Engage in imaginative play with small world resources
- Link play to experiences in other parts of their lives
- Comparing size, sorting, ordering, understanding space and position
- Deciding how to build and create a scene
- Solving problems by trial and error
- Use books or a computer to find out about animals, dinosaurs, jobs etc.

Resources	Organisation
• Small world buildings e.g. dolls house, garage, farm etc. • People, animals, fantasy figures etc… • Containers/trays to set scenes • Pieces of material to represent grass/garden/water • Small pieces of bark, pebbles, gravel, sand and other natural materials • Photographs of families, homes, people working in a garage • Pictures of dinosaurs, animals etc… • Non-fiction books • Story books	• Resources are clearly labelled and organised so that children can access them independently • Children are encouraged to use the resources in creative ways during independent play and focus activities • The space needs to be organised so that children are able to play in a focused way and to return to the activity if they wish • Children know that they are able to add resources from other areas if they wish

Year 1 Learning outcomes – Small World

Spoken Language:

- Listen and respond appropriately to adults and their peers
- Ask relevant questions to extend their understanding and knowledge
- Give well-structured descriptions, explanations and narratives for different purposes, including for expressing feelings
- Maintain attention and participate actively in collaborative conversations, staying on topic and initiating and responding to comments
- Use spoken language to develop understanding through speculating, hypothesising, imagining and exploring ideas

Mathematics:

- Sequence events in chronological order using language [for example, before and after, next, first, today, yesterday, tomorrow, morning, afternoon and evening]
- Describe position, direction and movement, including whole, half, quarter and three-quarter turns

Science and Geography:

- Identifying and classifying
- Identify and name a variety of common animals including fish, amphibians, reptiles, birds and mammals
- Use basic geographical vocabulary to refer to:
  - Key physical features, including: beach, cliff, coast, forest, hill, mountain, sea, ocean, river, soil, valley, vegetation, season and weather
  - Key human features, including: city, town, village, factory, farm, house, office, port, harbour and shop

Design and Technology:

- Generate, develop, model and communicate their ideas through talking, drawing, templates and mock ups

History:

- Acting out significant historical events and the lives of significant individuals in the past

What the children will do	What the adults will say and do
• Arrange resources to create a scene • Use their imagination to develop a storyline • Play together in a small group and share resources • Use resources carefully and respect what other children have done • Discuss what they are doing and what is happening • Find out about different types of animals, jobs that people do etc.	• Model language and actions • Follow lead given by the child • Withdraw where appropriate so that child can develop independence in this area of imaginative development and creative thinking • Develop and extend vocabulary – names of animals, vehicles, people and jobs, countries of the world, shops, farms, hospital, airport, garage etc. • Extend children's learning by asking open-ended questions • Can you tell me about the family who live here? • Why do you think this dinosaur has a long neck?

Figure 5.3 Small world prompt sheet

Resources

CASE STUDY

Resourcing Year 1 classrooms, in terms of both material and human resources can be challenging. Although the legal adult child ratio in Reception classes is one adult to 30 children, in practice almost all Reception classes we have encountered have at least one — and often two — additional teaching assistants. However, this is not always the case in Year 1. At Pickhurst Infant Academy in Bromley, a four-form entry school, all Year 1 classes have a teaching assistant for the morning session from Monday to Thursday, but in the afternoons and all day Friday there is just one teacher for each class. The four classes share a fairly small outdoor learning area, but a huge amount of thought and planning goes into the setting up in order to ensure children benefit from high quality learning experiences.

Teachers plan the week together, timetabling who will be indoors and who will be outside and when they teach whole-class inputs, guided groups and continuous provision. Planning is flexible and frequently adapted and adjusted depending on how children respond to the learning activities and experiences provided. The school recognises the crucial role of the adult in supporting continuous provision so when there are no additional adults, provision consists of short whole-class sessions and carefully planned continuous provision, rather than guided groups. Allocating an adult to facilitate continuous provision means children understand it is as important a part of their learning as when they are working with an adult in a small group. Although playing independently, their play is valued and they know adults are interested and — hopefully — interacting, where appropriate, in a meaningful positive way.

In terms of resources in the classroom, teachers at Pickhurst Infant Academy are careful to ensure that the activities provided enable children to build on and develop the skills they already possess. Assessing where children are developmentally is crucial — it is of little use knowing that a child at the end of EYFS is working towards a particular goal — all adults working with that child need to know what she can do. For example, the Early Learning Goal for "Understanding" requires that "Children follow instructions involving several ideas or actions. They answer how and why questions about their experiences and in response to stories or events" (DfE 2017). A child who has not met that goal, but who can show he understands conversations with others by his responses and can follow a simple instruction will need different support and provision from a child who is at the stage where she can respond to an instruction only when given visual clues.

> *One of the biggest challenges faced by teachers at Pickhurst Infant Academy was how to ensure that the independent learning activities set up for the children provided a high level of challenge and that skills development was progressive. Teachers recognise that subject knowledge is crucial in planning for progression of skills; they take time to model how to use the resources available, so for example, in woodwork, children have to learn how to use a vice, a fretsaw and other tools safely and accurately.*

It is important for schools to understand that resourcing a classroom does not necessarily involve a lot of expense. Children love natural materials; leaves, shells, twigs, stones, feathers and grasses can be placed in a builder's tray with magnifying glasses, tweezers, balance scales and writing implements, as prompts for investigation. Different-sized cardboard boxes, tubes, materials and large sheets of paper lend themselves perfectly to large-scale model and den making. These resources just need to be sourced and stored and can provide hours of purposeful independent play. One school knew that their children loved small world play; they extended this by making a class set of "mini me's." A small photograph of each child was stuck on to a cube and children thoroughly enjoyed re-enacting scenarios from well-known stories and including themselves and their friends.

Teacher workload

Organising a play-based curriculum and setting up imaginative and inviting indoor and outdoor learning areas which relate to children's interests are clearly time-consuming activities. If teaching a specific Year 1 Maths objective such as "add and subtract one-digit and two digit numbers to twenty, including zero" (DfE 2013), it can be tempting for busy teachers to teach the skill and provide a set of worksheets. In the example shown (Figure 5.4), it takes more time to source, wrap and label the paper cups with the numbers 1 to 10, set up the activity, prepare the instructions in how to knock down the tins with a beanbag and then add the total than to prepare a set of worksheets! However, this activity also supports children's social development in turn taking, gross and fine motor control and hand–eye co-ordination. It is also a lot more fun!

Figure 5.4 Practical maths activity

We have seen consistently high levels of concentration, motivation and engagement when there is a meaningful context for, and active involvement in, learning.

In the example given in the introduction, Lucy's delight was evident as she used a number line to solve a subtraction sum 13 − 5 and then used the key labelled with the number 8 to unlock the padlock to free her favourite superhero. Preparing a number of superhero characters, all of whom had subtraction problems and padlocks attached and labelling keys with numbers to release the padlocks, clearly took time; however, Karen the teacher explained that it was much easier to keep children on task, engaged and involved by providing this sort of playful learning environment than it would have been by getting children to sit at tables completing a series of "sums" which appeared to have little relevance to their lives.

Twenty years ago, in her book *Unlocking Formative Assessment*, Shirley Clarke was advocating the importance of putting learning into context. Throughout the book, she gives a number of examples, such as how learning about doubling and halving will help children in everyday life, when shopping for two of the same thing. She explains that recognising numbers from 1 to 10 is important for children because they will need to know numbers on buses and on doors (Clarke 2001). This principle of putting learning into a real life context is well supported in a play-based learning environment and is further developed in Chapter 7.

Summary

This chapter has considered some of the barriers in continuing to develop a play-based approach to learning in Year 1 and beyond. The external pressures, such as Ofsted and comparison of results of statutory assessments, are not going to go away and school leaders are understandably anxious not to risk falling results and adverse inspection outcomes. Implicit messages in documents such as *Bold Beginnings* which appear to encourage the adoption of more formal methods of teaching have not been helpful. However, a wealth of research, referred to in Chapter 2, as well as our own observations, indicates that there is little difference in the way children learn between the ages of five and six and that children thrive through first-hand learning experiences that are active, practical and hands-on. Resourcing a classroom with high-quality natural materials does not need a great deal of expense – just some time to collect and organise in accessible storage areas. We recognise that setting up a classroom with play-based resources is more time-consuming than sitting everyone on a carpet and then handing out worksheets, but the benefits of curious, happy motivated children keen to learn, clearly outweigh the disadvantages of demotivated, fidgety children and the behaviour problems that can result.

REFLECTIONS

For many teachers and parents, the move from EYFS into Year 1 signals the end of play-based curriculum and a move to more formal teaching. How can we challenge perceptions of what teaching looks like in Year 1 and help colleagues understand that the Characteristics of Effective Learning should underpin teaching and learning beyond EYFS?

References

Bradbury, A. and Roberts-Holmes, G. (2016) *"They are children, not robots." The introduction of Baseline Assessment*. London: ATL/NUT.

Bradbury, A. and Roberts-Holmes, G. (2017) *Grouping in Early Years and Key Stage 1 – A Necessary Evil*, National Education Union, reference 279/1117.

Clarke, S. (2001) *Unlocking Formative Assessment*, p. 27. London: Hodder and Stoughton.

Clarke, S. (2014) *Outstanding Formative Assessment Culture and Practice*. London: Hodder and Stoughton.

Department for Education (DfE) (2013) *The National Curriculum in England*, reference DfE-00178-2013. London: DfE.

Department for Education (DfE) (2017) *Statutory Framework for the Early Years Foundation Stage*, reference DfE-00169-2017. London: DfE.

Fisher, J. (2010) *Moving on to Key Stage 1 – Improving Transition from the Early Years Foundation Stage*. Berkshire: Open University Press.

Kangas, J., Ojala, M. and Venninen, T. (2015) Children's self-regulation in the context of participatory pedagogy in early childhood education, *Early Education and Development* 26(5–6): 847–870.

More Than a Score (2018) *Baseline Assessment: Why It Doesn't Add Up*. Available at www.morethanascore.org.uk (Accessed 26 August 2019).

Ofsted (2017) *Bold Beginnings: The Reception Curriculum in a Sample of Good and Outstanding Primary Schools*, November 2017, No. 170045. Manchester: Ofsted.

Ofsted (2019) *The Education Inspection Framework*. Manchester: Ofsted.

Parsons, S. and S. Hallam (2014). The impact of streaming on attainment at age seven: evidence from the Millennium Cohort Study. *Oxford Review of Education* 40(5): 567–589.

Phillips and Stipek (1993) Early formal schooling: Are we promoting achievement or anxiety? *Applied and Preventive Psychology: Current Scientific Directions* 2(3): 141–150.

Scherer, L. (2016). 'I am not clever, they are cleverer than us': Children reading in the primary school. *British Journal of Sociology of Education* 37(3): 389–407.

Spielman, A. (2018) *Phase 3 of Research into the School Curriculum*, published 11 December 2018. https://www.gov.uk/government/.../commentary-on-curriculum-research-phase-3 (Accessed 17 July 2019).

Sutton Trust (2011) *Education Endowment Foundation Teaching and Learning Toolkit.*

TACTYC (2017) *Bald Beginnings -A Response to Ofsted's (2017) Report, Bold Beginnings: The Reception Curriculum in a Sample of Good and Outstanding Primary Schools*, by TACTYC (Association for Professional Development in Early Years). December 2017. Available at www.tactyc.org.uk (Accessed 26 August 2019).

6 Transitions

Periods of change can make any of us feel vulnerable and so it is essential that children are well prepared for transition at any stage in their education so their experience is as positive as possible. When schools prepare and understand transition, children are more likely to feel secure and settle more easily into their new environment. This is particularly important for children with additional needs. Many people underestimate the impact of transition from Reception to Year 1; they make the point that children are familiar with the building, the adults and know their classmates; it is not as though they are starting school for the first time. However, to a child, who has been away from school for the six weeks' summer holiday, the changes can appear huge. They are possibly entering the school by a different gate, there will be different arrangements for leaving their parents and carers and they will be finding their way to a new classroom, almost certainly with a new teacher. They may not be sure of where to leave their coats, their lunchboxes, where the Year 1 toilets are situated and whether they will need to ask permission to go to the toilet. They will have to cope with the hustle and bustle of playtimes and arrangements for lunchtimes may well be different. This is all in addition to any changes to the classroom environment and the way teaching might be delivered! However, all these worries can be minimised by effective transition policies and procedures.

We asked EYFS teachers, Year 1 teachers, parents and children about their perceptions and experiences of transition. This research was carried out using questionnaires with parents and teachers and holding conversations in small groups with children.

Teachers

Teachers were asked: "What do you think the difference is between teaching in Reception and Year 1?" They all recognised that, whereas the Reception classes are able to tailor the curriculum around the children's interests, in Year 1, the day is more structured and has more teacher-led activities because of the need to fit in National Curriculum subjects such as Science and PE into the timetable. Reception teachers were genuinely concerned that the independence and autonomy developed in children across the Early Years Foundation Stage (EYFS) would inevitably be compromised because of the move to more adult-directed activities and a structured daily timetable. They knew that in Year 1, children spend a greater proportion of time sitting down on the carpet and at table-based activities, especially for Mathematics and literacy, and were worried that not all children were ready for this. Early Years teachers were aware that in many schools there is little space for the children in Year 1, therefore limiting opportunities for sustained play and reducing the freedom to move inside and outside. Reception classes have environments which promote active play-based learning; children are able to move around and, in most cases, choose how, when and where to explore and discover.

Teachers in both year groups felt there was significant pressure in Year 1, especially after Christmas to "get the children ready for Year 2." They saw this as a concern when children have only very recently moved from the free flow environment of the Reception class.

Recognising concerns of parents

When asked: "What do you think is important for effective transition from Reception to Year 1?", teachers came up with a number of very similar responses. Top of everyone's list was the recognition that many parents struggled with transition. One teacher commented: "In Year R, we build a strong relationship with the families as we are able to do home visits and are on the door both morning and after school to chat with the parents." She went on to explain that many parents had mentioned that, although they understood the need to promote independence by letting their children go into school on their own, they had found it difficult as their children moved through the school, to know what they had been up to throughout the day. Teachers went on to talk about the importance of continuing a strong partnership with parents, throughout Year 1 and beyond, with regular updates and communication.

Getting to know the children

The second common theme was the importance of Year 1 teachers getting to know the children before they start in September. One teacher commented that before children start in the Reception class, their teachers spend time getting to know them through home visits and sometimes part-time to full-time transition to school. Reception staff felt that transition would be eased if Year 1 teachers and teaching assistants could spend time in the EYFS classrooms, during the summer term. This could be reading a story at the end of the day or joining the children during free flow and child-initiated learning sessions. Staff would use this time to build relationships in an environment where the children are already confident. Obviously, this is more difficult if Year 1 teachers are going to be new to the school but for staff who are already working in the school, this should be reasonably straightforward to organise.

Familiarity of routines

The third main area identified by all the teachers was the importance of continuing, as far as possible, with the routines to which children are accustomed,. One Year 1 teacher commented: "Many children find the transition overwhelming and aren't ready to be sat at a table for long periods." Another said: "Children can be vulnerable when there is change; this will impact them emotionally, particularly those with Special Educational Needs and Disabilities. It's important to prepare them for the change keeping thing similar and settle them into a familiar environment so it does not negatively impact on their learning. I believe that we work so hard in EYFS on the children's Personal, Social and Emotional Development but without a smooth transition all this can be undone. It can easily be forgotten that the children are still only five years old and any change in routine can completely unsettle them."

Curriculum coverage

CASE STUDY

One teacher we spoke to, from Allen Edwards Primary School, an inner-city school in central London, was highly appreciative of the support of her EYFS colleagues. Although she was experienced in teaching older children, last September was the first time she had ever been given a Year 1 class. Understanding the importance of a smooth transition, she set up the classroom to mirror that of the Reception Class. However, she was initially somewhat alarmed as children set off to explore the activities she had set up for them and asked the EYFS lead who was supporting her: "What is going on? This is chaos!" Having been used to very clear structures and routines of delivering an input on the carpet then sending children off to complete work at their tables in their exercise books, she was at first unsure what the children could possibly be learning and how she was going to get them to meet the objectives set out in the National Curriculum Year 1 programme of study. Fortunately, the school was able to arrange for the EYFS lead to spend some time working alongside her for the first few days. Under the guidance of her EYFS colleagues she quickly began to recognise the learning opportunities that arose over the course of the day. Being a highly reflective teacher, she came to realise that whereas in the past she would have planned exactly what she wanted to cover

> *in each subject each day, this way of working gave her and the children far more flexibility; it didn't matter if not everyone accessed a specific learning focus at the same time and it was much better to go with children's interests. What she found particularly rewarding was that by halfway through the year she felt she knew this group of children much better than any class she had ever taught, because as well as working with each child regularly and intensively in small groups, she had been able to take time to interact with them as they played and to observe each of them really closely.*

A particular challenge initially for her was the worry of how to ensure coverage of all of the Year 1 curriculum, but over the course of the first few months she realised how much of the curriculum could be covered through independent learning activities planned as part of the continuous provision. For example, the subject content for Art and Design in Key Stage 1 includes:

- To use a range of materials creatively to design and make products

- To use drawing, painting and sculpture to develop and share their ideas, experiences and imagination

- To develop a wide range of art and design techniques in using colour, pattern, texture, line, shape, form and space.

Children are likely to have far fewer opportunities to consolidate, revisit and develop these skills if Art and Design is taught as a whole-class lesson once a week or a fortnight; however, having an Art and Design workshop available every day means children can become more proficient in each of these areas, whilst exploring, practising, making mistakes and embedding their skills.

Similarly, an overarching topic of Traditional Tales gives many opportunities to use basic geographical vocabulary referring to key physical and human features. Any of these tales such as *Little Red Riding Hood, Hansel and Gretel, The Three Little Pigs, Goldilocks and the Three Bears* or *The Gingerbread Man* easily lend themselves to teaching the skill of devising a simple map and using and constructing basic symbols. The beauty of developing these skills as part of continuous provision means that they can be revisited and consolidated time and time again within a meaningful context, rather than as a one-off lesson, the content of which may well soon be forgotten.

We asked teachers to identify what they felt were the biggest barriers when teaching in Year 1. Staff came up with a number of responses. These included: "From experience I don't think the teachers know the children well enough before starting Year 1." Others commented on how children struggled with the transition to a more formal way of working with timetabled subjects. Other responses referred to the pressure experienced by many Year 1 teachers in trying to strike a balance between continuing to develop children's love of learning by allowing them some autonomy whilst at the same time fitting in all the discrete, unrelated subjects in the Year 1 National Curriculum and getting them ready for the Year 1 Phonic Screening Check and SATs in Year 2.

Parents

Many schools within the Swale Academies Trust hold a transition week towards the end of the summer term, when children go their new classrooms and get to know their new teachers and support staff. At the end of this week, we sent out a questionnaire to parents to see how they felt about their children moving from EYFS to Year 1.

We asked them:

- What has your son/daughter enjoyed in Reception this year?

- As a parent, what has been your experience of Reception this year?

- How are you and your son/daughter feeling about moving to Year 1?

- How did your son/daughter settle into Year 1 during their transition week?

- If you have any more information that you would like to share about your son/daughter moving to Year 1, please share.

The majority of parents commented on how the staff in the Reception classes had been "fantastic", they said that the staff were always welcoming, happy to help and caring. When children started school in EYFS, parents really put their trust into the Reception teachers as it was their first experience of school life. Building strong relationships between staff and parents is a key aspect of the EYFS and it had been noted as a huge positive from parents.

EYFS teachers had offered a range of different ways to get parents into school to work alongside their child. These included stay and play sessions, where parents were invited into engage in the free flow learning environment and learn alongside their child. Parents were able to get to know the staff, to see how and what the children were learning as well as get involved with some of the activities. This helped them to understand the way children are taught which in most cases was very different from their own recollections of how they had been taught.

When asked how parents felt about their child moving to Year 1 and beyond, many said they were slightly anxious about the change, highlighting to us why it is so important for consistency between the sorts of experiences children have in Term 6 in EYFS and Term 1 in Year 1. Parents stated that the children were excited to move to Year 1 but would miss their teachers and were "sad about not having the outside space." Again, this further emphasises the desirability for Year 1 children to have their own outside area in some shape or form. After initial nerves from both parents and children at the start of transition week, the children thoroughly enjoyed their transition week according to these parental questionnaires. This is because Year 1 mirrored the EYFS timetable and continued with the topic they were learning in their EYFS classrooms. The only major changes were the new teachers and the actual classroom, although it was set up in a very similar way to what the children were used to in their EYFS classrooms.

Parents at schools within the Swale Academies Trust were highly appreciative of the wealth of information provided by the school about the transition from Reception into Year 1. This included open days, information-sharing events, newsletters, "meet the teacher" drop-ins and website updates.

Some parents with older children commented on how they were initially apprehensive about their children moving into Year 1; they remembered their older children worrying about whether they would be allowed to go to the toilet, whether they would still be with their friends and if the work would be too difficult. They were reassured by the school's determination to include them in the transition process and the similarity of approach at the start of the year.

Children

The following extracts are examples of what children wrote to their new teachers to tell them what they had enjoyed in Reception (Figures 6.1 and 6.2).

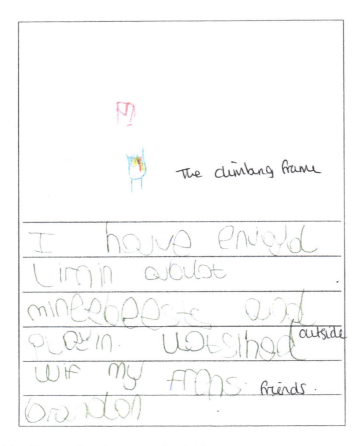

Figure 6.1 What I have enjoyed most at school this year

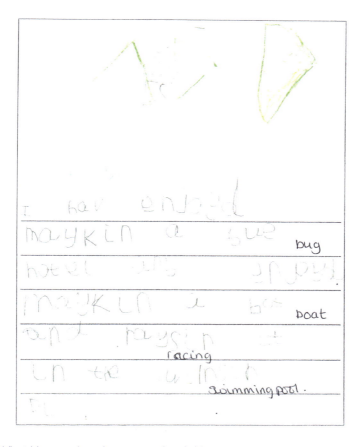

Figure 6.2 What I have enjoyed most at school this year

After the children had been in Year 1 for a term or so, we asked them how they felt about being in their new year group. We were really pleased by the positive responses which included:

> "I like the creative zone where we can make lots of different things"
> "It is just like Reception but we have different teachers"
> "The work is a bit harder than Ruby class, but it is fun"
> "I like the outside area where we can do lots of maths"
> "Year 1 is fun, I like being with my friends and we learn together"

Looking closely at some of these comments, we can see that these children's experiences reflect the school's commitment to providing a smooth transition from Reception to Year 1 by keeping the environment and the activities as similar as possible to what the children were used to. The reference to the creative zone shows that this important aspect of continuous provision is available to children and the comment "We can make lots of different things" suggests that there is an element of choice and that activities in that area are open-ended. It was good to see that teachers do not restrict Mathematics to the classroom, but that they are making the most of the mathematical opportunities available in the outdoor learning area. The comment "The work is a bit harder than Ruby class, but it is fun" indicates that this child recognises that the work is more challenging, but also suggests this child is confident, resilient and relaxed.

These comments are in stark contrast to the experiences recorded by the two boys in the NFER research project referred to in Chapter 2, who struggled with the transition and complained that they were wasting their lives because of the time they spent sitting on the carpet!

How transition works at Westlands Primary School

We have already discussed the importance of involving parents in the transition process, the need for Year 1 staff to get to know their children before they start in Year 1 and the importance of maintaining systems and routines as far as possible. So what does the whole process look like in practice?

Once the teachers for Year 1 have been agreed, ideally at the latest by early June once resignation dates have passed (and we do realise this is not always easy!) work on transition should start. We draw up an action plan which identifies tasks, people responsible and timelines. This is then circulated amongst all current EYFS staff and those who will be teaching in Year 1. A copy of a typical transition action plan is provided at Figure 6.3, along with a blank proforma, Figure 6.4. Schools are free to use and adapt these proformas as they wish.

Using EYFS profile data to plan for Year 1

One of the first activities is for EYFS and Year 1 staff to carry out moderation of work for children in the Reception class in Term 6. This ensures there is an agreed judgement of EYFS end of year assessments, especially with reading, writing and Mathematics. Staff across both year groups should be confident in their understanding of the Early Learning Goals (ELGs) and what is meant by a Good Level of Development (GLD). It is really important that Year 1 teachers delve deeply into the data as headline percentages of the proportion of children achieving GLD can be misleading. Some children who have been assessed as working at the expected standard in reading, writing and Mathematics may not have achieved GLD, either because they have not yet met the expected standard

Tasks	People responsible	Timelines	Impact
Set up transition day/ week, once teachers are identified for Year 1	SLT	Towards the end of the Summer term	Dates for transition events confirmed and arrangements finalised. Children get to know new teacher and new classroom.
Arrange "meet the teacher" drop ins for parents	DHT	July	Dates confirmed. Year 1 staff confident to meet with parents approaches to eaching and learning in Year 1
Gather information from the previous teacher and teaching assistant. Set up EYFS and Year 1 staff to jointly moderate children's work. Year 1 staff to spend time in Yr R getting to know the children.	EYFS/ Year 1 leads	Transition meetings June	Year 1 staff understand outcomes of EYFS profile assessments and know the children's interests. Moderation judgements agreed.
Arrange for Year 1 and EYFS teachers to plan together at the start of the year taking into account the characteristics of effective learning	EYFS/ Year 1 leads	September	EYFS staff support teachers with planning for the first week or two. Characteristics of effective learning planned for and evident in practice
Plan the learning environment and resources using information from the children and teachers to support the children's interests and mirror EYFS at the start of Year 1 Classroom environment, including outdoors, set up to encourage independence and exploration as in EYFS.	All year 1 staff (with support from EYFS lead)	September onwards	Enabling environment created that allows children to demonstrate what they can do. Staff understand the crucial role of play. Children can access resources and return them independently. If possible, rolling snack bar in place. Some free flow opportunities to include outdoor learning.
Identify vulnerable children and those with identified needs in preparing for transition from EYFS - Year 1	EYFS staff and SENDCo	July and reviewed regularly across the	Vulnerable children identified and well supported – making progress from starting points.
Reassess any children not achieving a Good Level of Development in October and for any children still not meeting the standard, in December.	Year 1 lead and SENDCo	October December	Any child who has not met the Good Level of Development by December of Year 1 may have underlying special educational needs and disabilities and so require need additional support
Review systems for maintaining and cementing positive relationships with parents	Year 1 lead	On going	Information meetings for parents held early in the Autumn term. Parent feedback is positive. Workshops such as maths/phonics planned
Identify any training needs for adults working in Year 1	SLT and EYFS and Year 1 leads	On going	All adults effectively managed and deployed They understand how to support children's play/learning

Figure 6.3 Transition action plan

Tasks	People responsible	Timelines	Impact

Figure 6.4 Blank transition action plan

in aspects of their Personal, Social and Emotional Development (PSED) or their physical skills. If Year 1 staff just look at the GLD results, it could mean that work planned in English and Mathematics is insufficiently challenging for some children, and, more importantly, that PSED needs for all children are given insufficient attention.

We cannot overemphasise how important it is for Year 1 staff to understand the data gathered at the end of EYFS. By discussing these judgements with Reception staff, it is much easier to plan appropriate next steps for groups and individuals. This is the same for children who are judged as "exceeding" in some areas of development; teachers need to ensure the next steps are challenging enough for these children. We recommend that children who have not achieved GLD by the end of Reception (often because they are summer born and not yet five years old when these assessments are carried out towards the end of May and early June) are reassessed in October and then again at Christmas.

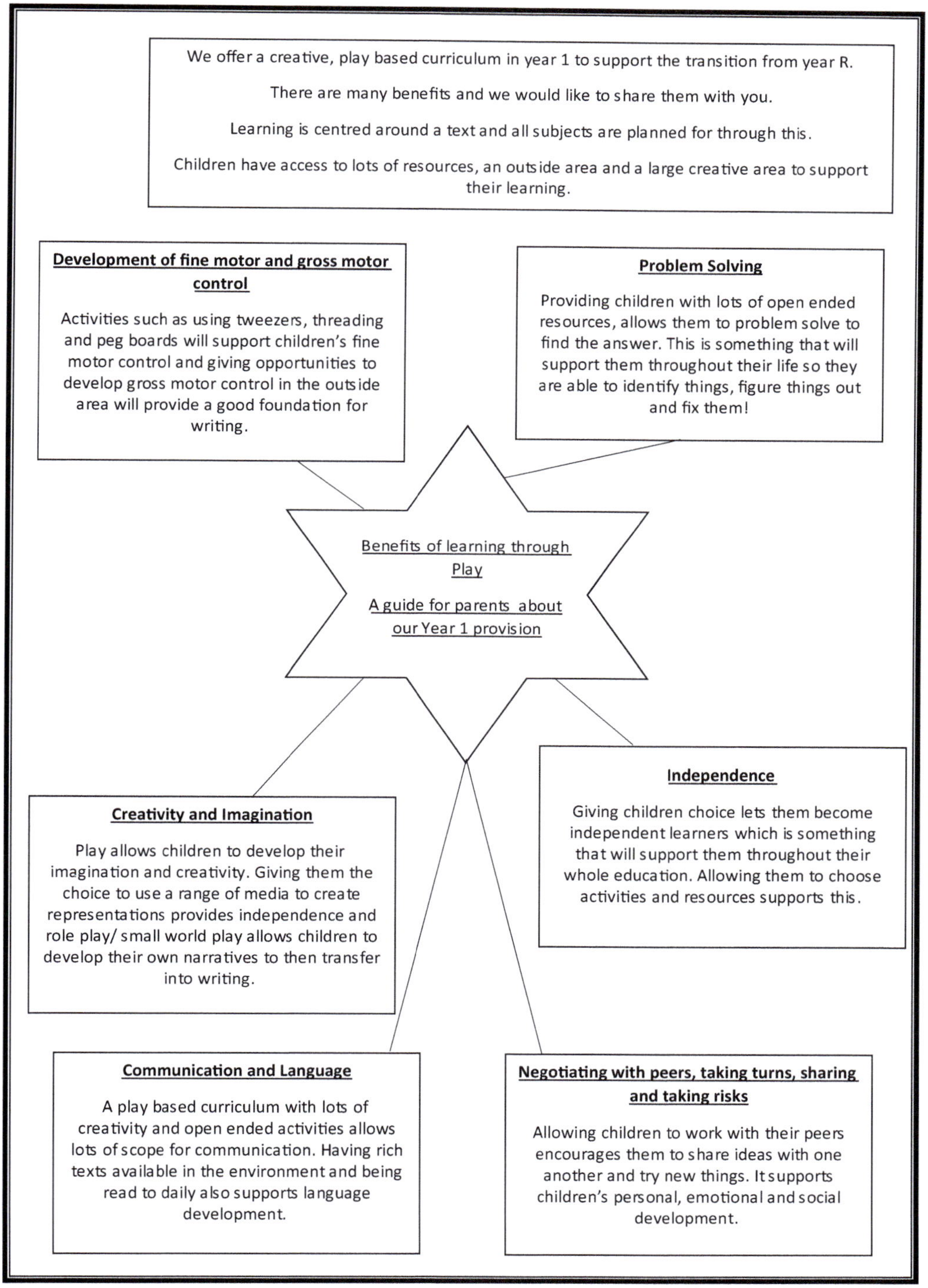

We offer a creative, play based curriculum in year 1 to support the transition from year R.

There are many benefits and we would like to share them with you.

Learning is centred around a text and all subjects are planned for through this.

Children have access to lots of resources, an outside area and a large creative area to support their learning.

Development of fine motor and gross motor control

Activities such as using tweezers, threading and peg boards will support children's fine motor control and giving opportunities to develop gross motor control in the outside area will provide a good foundation for writing.

Problem Solving

Providing children with lots of open ended resources, allows them to problem solve to find the answer. This is something that will support them throughout their life so they are able to identify things, figure things out and fix them!

Benefits of learning through Play

A guide for parents about our Year 1 provision

Creativity and Imagination

Play allows children to develop their imagination and creativity. Giving them the choice to use a range of media to create representations provides independence and role play/ small world play allows children to develop their own narratives to then transfer into writing.

Independence

Giving children choice lets them become independent learners which is something that will support them throughout their whole education. Allowing them to choose activities and resources supports this.

Communication and Language

A play based curriculum with lots of creativity and open ended activities allows lots of scope for communication. Having rich texts available in the environment and being read to daily also supports language development.

Negotiating with peers, taking turns, sharing and taking risks

Allowing children to work with their peers encourages them to share ideas with one another and try new things. It supports children's personal, emotional and social development.

Figure 6.5 Leaflet for parents – play-based learning

108   Transitions

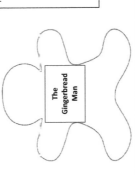

Writing Opportunities
Use outlines of a Gingerbread man to write descriptive words in to describe the characters, children to then write descriptive sentences
Re-tell the story by writing own book - have blank books readily available for the children to-children can us felt tip pens, colouring pencils and pencils. They can illustrate this themselves. Children to use adjectives to describe. They can design their own front cover
Writing instructions on how to make a gingerbread man.
Write an alternative ending to the story.
English objective -Sequencing sentences to form short narratives re-reading what they have written to check that it makes sense

Geography
Create maps to show the Gingerbread man's route. Children to use positional language and compass directions to explain the journey the gingerbread man will make.
Geography objective -use simple compass directions (North, South, East and West) and locational and directional language [for example, near and far; left and right], to describe the location of features and routes on a map

ICT
Create a beebot mat with different parts of the story – children to programme the beebotto move to a certain part of the mat, when it reaches that part children to describe what happens
Computing objective - recognise common uses of information technology beyond school

Outside area
Give children a variety of materials to choose from and work out which would be best to create a bridge for the gingerbread man to use to cross the river. Large resources to be available as this is outside.
Children to build the little lady's house.
Children to create large gingerbread men using different shapes. One more and one less than a number using the buttons on the gingerbread man.
Science objective - identify and name a variety of everyday materials, including wood, plastic, glass, metal, water, and rock describe the simple physical properties of a variety of everyday materials
Geometry properties of shapes - recognise and name common 2-D and 3-D shapes, including: 2-D shapes [for example, rectangles (including squares), circles and triangles], 3-D shapes [for example, cuboids (including cubes), pyramids and spheres].
Measurement objective - Pupils should compare, describe and solve practical problems for: lengths and heights [for example, long/short, longer/shorter, tall/short, double/half]
Number and Place Value; given a number, identify one more and one less
Large stage for role play for children to re - tell the story
Writing tool kits for children to write the story

Art and DT
Children to create the little old lady's house. Children to create their own gingerbread men using different media.
Children to paint different scenes of the story.
Children to cook their own gingerbread men.
Children to create a bridge for the gingerbread man to use to cross the river instead of having to swim.
Art and Design objective - to use a range of materials creatively to design and make products to develop a wide range of art and design techniques in using colour, pattern, texture, line, shape, form and space select from and use a wide range of materials and components, including construction materials, textiles and ingredients, according to their characteristics build structures, exploring how they can be made stronger, stiffer and more stable

Communication and Language/ role play
Tuff spots with small world play for children to re-tell the story – can you create your own ending? Can you use resources to create the setting of the story?
Tuff spots with different ingredients in for children to explore and discuss. What happens if we add water to the flour and mix it together?
Children to create their own masks to re tell the story
Spoken language objective - participate in discussions, presentations, performances, role play

Music
Have a range of musical instruments available or the children to use to re-tell the story through role play – what instrument will you use to show the gingerbread man running?
Music objective - use their voices expressively and creatively by singing songs and speaking chants and rhymes play tuned and untuned instruments musically

Figure 6.6 Leaflet for parents – planning around a core text

Transition information for parents

Next, we organise a transition meeting for parents before children move to Year 1. This gives parents the chance to meet new teachers and teaching assistants, to look around the new environments and discuss the expectations of Year 1 and end of year assessments. If a play-based learning approach is adopted in Year 1, the pedagogy behind it can be shared with parents. At those meetings we explain the benefits of play and the importance of continuing to develop fine and gross motor skills, independence, problem solving, creativity and imagination. We also explain how we plan the learning around a core text and how we ensure full coverage of the Key Stage 1, Year 1 curriculum. Figures 6.5 and 6.6 are examples of the information we give to parents. Schools are free to use or adapt these resources as they wish.

Transition arrangements within school

At the end of each academic year, handover meetings happen between different year groups. These are extremely important to ensure all information is shared with new teachers. During these meetings, data should be shared as well as children's interests and likes or dislikes. This should then feed into planning. Giving staff time to plan with EYFS teachers is helpful as they will be able to share all of this information. One of the things we do during Term 6 is get children to paint or draw a picture of something they have really enjoyed doing at school and either label it or add a piece of writing. This is then sent to the new teacher to support planning. Staff should also remind themselves of the *Characteristics of Effective Learning*, set out in the Statutory Framework for the Early Years Foundation Stage (2018), and how best to plan for these. It is good practice that these should form the start of any planning session.

During Term 6, schools usually have a transition day, morning or afternoon – some schools even have a transition week. As discussed in Chapter 3, enabling environments are key to transition so having Year 1 classrooms set up in a similar way to the EYFS classrooms can really help. Since introducing a play-based approach to Year 1, our children have definitely coped better with transitions because conditions are similar and changes take place over a period of time. Year 1 classrooms should, where possible, look like the EYFS classrooms at the start of the academic year. Staff may need to be creative with their space if the classrooms are smaller, but this can be done with a little imagination – and help from EYFS staff!

During transition time, whether it is for half a day, a whole day or a week, teachers discuss with the children what they have enjoyed learning in EYFS and what topics they would like to focus on in Year 1. Giving children the time to discuss their interests makes them feel valued and planning a topic for Term 1 that is centred around their interests means levels of engagement will be higher. One of our teachers spoke about the importance of bringing the learning to the child and matching the curriculum to children's interests. This will change year on year and no two years will be the same because children are different. Teachers should have the confidence to change planning where they see fit to suit the needs of all children as they are individuals. Free flow learning means that children will get the opportunity to work in mixed ability pairs to support one another, small groups with an adult or even 1:1 with an adult in the provision.

During Term 6, we arrange for Year 1 teachers to go into the Reception classes when possible, to read stories and to observe and join in free flow in order to get to know the children.

One of the things that our EYFS staff do very well is to plan enrichment activities. This is something that Year 1 staff have continued to do as creating a "hook" at the start of the term is really effective in engaging all children. Equally, a memorable event to celebrate the end of a topic and to bring together all of the skills and knowledge that have been acquired over a term, can be something children – and their parents, if involved, are likely to remember for many years to come. In one of our schools, children held a carnival as part of their work on festivals and another memorable experience was a pirate party.

Many schools expect Year 1 children to attend all whole-school assemblies – whilst this can be an important way of creating a sense of belonging to a large community, we would question the value, certainly at the beginning of the year, of insisting that all Year 1 children attend all assemblies. This may be something that will need to be negotiated with senior staff; it may be possible for children to attend perhaps one whole school assembly and a Key Stage 1 assembly each week for the first term, gradually building up over the year. It could be that specific children will have to be withdrawn if they cannot cope with the expectations of sitting and listening quietly for any length of time.

Summary

Transitions between all year groups in a school, not just Reception to Year 1, can be eased by careful planning, sharing of information and strong lines of communication between parents, carers and professionals. As we have discussed, the role of the parent is especially important during this time and schools who value the partnership with parents and carers are likely to find the transition process runs smoothly.

REFLECTION

How does transition work in your school? Which of these do you already do and what might you add?

- Create a transition action plan
- Identify teachers for Year 1 as early as possible
- Arrange moderation of work with EYFS and Year 1 teachers
- Arrange for Year 1 staff to spend time in EYFS
- Set up transition meeting for parents with new staff
- Hold effective handover meetings
- Staff to discuss children's interests to inform planning
- EYFS staff to support Term 1 planning with Year 1 staff
- Year 1 teaching assistants to spend time in the reception classes during free flow to establish relationships
- Children produce a piece of work about themselves and send it to their new teacher – this work can then be displayed in the new classroom for when children start in Year 1.

Reference

Department for Education (2018) *Statutory Framework for the Early Years Foundation Stage.* Available at https://www.gov.uk/government/publications/early-years-foundation-stage-framework--2 (Accessed 11 March 2019).

7 Moving forward – Year 1 and beyond

We started our work in extending a play-based approach from EYFS into Year 1 because we knew that an abrupt transition to a formal way of working as soon as children start Year 1 was not right. However, changing practice was not always straightforward and needed work to win over hearts and minds as well as to challenge perceptions of what teaching in Year 1 should look like. In order to embed practice and ensure the approach is not dependent on the talents and skills of individual staff, we have had to make sure the principles of our approach are well founded and clearly communicated across the Trust.

The importance of play

As Michael Rosen points out: "Simply by using the word 'play', we often make it seem less important than, say, education, work, knowledge, or 'real' learning – whatever that is. After all, the word 'play' has emotional and historical links to words like 'idleness', 'escapism', 'frivolity', 'leisure' and various kinds of 'pointlessness'. Education and learning on the other hand are (we often tell ourselves) serious and important." He goes on to say "It's not as simple as that – play is fundamental to our development as people and more broadly, as a society and culture" (Rosen 2019).

What we have learned is the crucial importance of strong, supportive leadership. Our leaders across the Trust know that when children start in Year 1, they are still just five years old and are aware from experience that formalising learning for very young children can put them off learning and school in general. We know that in many schools there is a misconception that formal learning produces higher standards and it is important to tackle that perception. Where play-based learning is embedded in Year 1 and staff are committed to the approach, constantly assessing children through observation and discussion, then planning appropriate activities for them to make progress, standards are high. In our schools where this is in place, at the end of the year the proportions meeting at least the expected levels for their year group are broadly in line with those reaching a Good Level of Development in EYFS. This is in contrast to the situation experienced in some schools where the proportion of children meeting age-related expectations dips in Year 1, especially in writing.

Child development theories which were discussed in Chapter 2 indicate that by the age of seven, most children are able to cope with the demands of a more traditional curriculum but we were keen to explore how to retain specific elements of a curriculum that enthused and engaged children as they move through the school. We were certain that the principles outlined in the Characteristics of Effective Learning, which underpin pedagogy in the Early Years and were referred to in earlier chapters were equally relevant to older children.

Much of the material in this chapter has been drawn from the work that has been developed at James Dixon Primary School, an inner-city school in south-east London and a member of the Swale Academies Trust. We are grateful to the executive headteacher and staff and particularly Fred Banks, the assistant headteacher, part of whose responsibility is to develop outdoor learning across all year groups, for their contributions.

Putting learning in context

Contextualising learning is a key aspect of the curriculum at James Dixon Primary School.

When children have the opportunity to link new learning to something they already know and understand, this learning takes on a deeper meaning; therefore, they are much more likely to retain it. Many schools have recognised this and in devising their own bespoke curricula, have linked much of the work, especially in the foundation subjects. At James Dixon Primary, wherever possible, foundation subjects as well as some English lessons, are linked to the overarching theme. For example in Year 6 the theme is "Native Americans and the Wild West."

The curriculum map explains:

- As Historians, we will study how the Native Americans lived before the arrival of Europeans and how lives both changed once they met.

- As Geographers, we will locate the Prairie states of North America.

- As Design Technologists, we will design and make traditional Tipis and dream catchers (linking cultural stories and beliefs).

- As Writers, we will use the text "Holes" by Louis Sachar as inspiration to write and create our own persuasive leaflets, descriptions of a setting, formal and informal letters and historical stories.

During the Spring term in Year 4, children learn about Vikings and Anglo Saxons.

- As Historians we will look at how Britain changed after the Viking invasion. We will look at the everyday life during Anglo-Saxon and Viking times and learn how it has influenced the country that we live in today.

- As Geographers, we will learn to read, understand and follow an Ordnance Survey map. We will also learn about the Anglo-Saxon and Viking vocabulary that is used for many of the place names in the United Kingdom.

- As Writers we will look at the features of myths and legends. We will plan our own setting, characters and plot to write our own Viking saga.

- In Art and Design, children design and make money containers using examples of Anglo-Saxon and Viking purses as inspiration.

In other schools, children have designed and made their own Viking shields which they then use to create and act out a shield wall.

Fred described how some activities such as cooking can be an excellent vehicle for contextualising – growing produce, devising and making recipes all have clear links to cross-curricular learning, including design technology, maths and science – as well as being fun.

He gave the example of learning about the Great Fire of London; children might be interested in listening to a teacher telling the story of Thomas Farriner's bakery in Pudding Lane. However, telling them about how the fire started in his bakery whilst children are making bread or biscuits is likely to be a far more memorable experience and will help consolidate and contextualise the story of the Great Fire of London.

Fred explained the importance of contextualising and consolidating learning so it makes sense to children. He pointed out that as adults, an action such as whispering can be interpreted differently based on contextual understanding. If we walked into a restaurant or bar and everyone was whispering we would think they were being rude, possibly talking about us. This would make us feel uncomfortable. But, if we were in a library or a hospital ward, whispering is what we would expect. So, by contextualising learning, we are trying to make sense of the situation.

Linking learning to high-quality core texts

Across all our schools, the overarching theme for the term is linked to a core text. So, for example, in one of our schools, pupils in Year 3, in the Spring first half term, have "Explorers" as an overall theme. There are a number of texts which support this theme, including *The Green Ship* by Quentin Blake (Blake 1998;) and *The Firework Maker's Daughter* by Philip Pullman.(Pullman 1995) Both stories feature an expedition and link with the geography focus of global geography, time zones, global resources and trade, art work based around fireworks, building transport structures for design technology and learning about mapping skills. A number of non-fiction texts, such as *Shackleton's Journey* by William Grill, (Grill 2014;) would also link well with the theme

Linking learning to a high-quality core text means all children have access to a rich range of literature which they sometimes would not be able to read for themselves. It is important for schools to continually review the texts they are using and make sure the text fits in and supports the topic – there is a need for a range of genres, information books, narratives, poetry, autobiographies, biographies. It is also important to include picture books across all year groups as these can be interpreted at different levels by children of different ages.

Learning outside the classroom

Being unconstrained by the walls of the classroom is really important for young children and at James Dixon Primary School, learning outside the classroom has a prominent role in the curriculum across all year groups. Fred explained that experiential learning that helps children reconnect with the outside world is really important for mental health.

Across all our schools, teachers are recognising the developing social media and peer group pressures arising at another important transition time – from Year 2 to Year 3 as a result of various levels of maturity during the change from Key Stage 1 to Key Stage 2. The outdoor learning opportunities which Forest School provide help children make social connections in the environment – how to cope with new thoughts, feelings and social friendships; in Forest School, children take control, teachers stand back. This allows children to find their place in class, to negotiate, socialise, engage in peer-based learning

CASE STUDY

Fred provided a powerful example of how experiential learning can make a difference for an individual child. During Year 6, a new pupil arrived from South America. He spoke no English and at first was finding it difficult to relate to his peers. In Forest School, his teacher realised he had already learned a number of skills from his time in South America, including gathering materials to light a fire and chopping wood, so encouraged him to do that. Other children started crowding round, watching him, and praising him. Because of this newly-won respect, the other children in the class started spending more time socially with him which meant his vocabulary grew and by the end of Year 6 he had made marked progress in language skills and reading and was able to produce a simple, legible piece of writing. Had that child not had the opportunity to demonstrate his skills and talents, it is likely he would have continued to feel isolated and taken a lot more time to settle in to school.

and to demonstrate individual talents and skills which support self-confidence and self-esteem. Forest School also provides opportunities to see the relationship between risks and benefits; children are taught to climb trees, light fires, use bow saws and chop wood; by Year 6, they are taught to use power drills. Risk to benefit assessments are drawn up and discussed and before children undertake a new activity they have a clear understanding how the benefits of an activity outweigh the risks and how they as individuals can mitigate those risks.

The James Dixon school website (https://www.jamesdixon.bromley.sch.uk) refers to the opportunities it provides for exploration, experience and risk taking through child-led learning. It states:

> *Making sense of the wide and wondrous world around us creates, motivates and develops links within our learning and personal development in ways the classroom environment cannot and we, at James Dixon, believe every child has the right and privilege to experience this as an essential part of their learning and personal development.*
>
> (https://www.jamesdixon.bromley.sch.uk)

At the school, there is an expectation that in every year group for every topic, some learning will take place outside the classroom. This could be an enrichment experience such as an educational visit or it could be the development and mastery of specific skills in an outdoor setting.

To give some examples; in Year 2, themes at different times of the year include Traditional Tales, Pirates and the Great Fire of London. When learning Traditional Tales, children use the outdoor learning environment to observe plants and how they grow. They also visit the local library to explore the world of books and listen to some traditional tales. Later in the year, learning about Pirates provides a wealth of opportunities to find treasure and create their own maps. They also have a themed pirate day which incorporates a range of outdoor learning activities, including walking the plank! Building models of houses that would have been in place at the time of the Great Fire of London then burning them (under controlled supervision!) allows children to gain a real understanding of how fire can spread and how this had such a devastating impact on London.

When Year 6 were learning about Native Americans and the Wild West, the outdoor learning element focussed on developing team-building and communication skills when working in small groups. Children explored Native American structures and created their own, using naturally sourced materials. They also focused on the importance of the land to Native Americans and how it influenced their way of life.

Many of these outdoor learning experiences are activities that are repeated in schools across the country at different times. What makes children's experiences at this school so special is the commitment that school leaders demonstrate to ensuring that opportunities to learn outdoors are non-negotiable and are woven across the curriculum for all age groups.

Enabling environments

Senior leaders at James Dixon Primary School were determined that learning environments should provide inspiration and aspiration. They recognised that as a staff they needed to unpick what was understood by "enabling environments" – and to appreciate it meant much more than what was provided in the traditional classroom. It was important to consider different approaches to learning, including the use of breakout areas and going outside to record work. This might involve changing the mindsets of some teachers! In many schools, as children move into Key Stage 2, almost all of the work, especially in English, Mathematics and Science, is recorded in exercise books. Whilst this can be a useful record of both coverage and progress, there are sometimes missed opportunities for children to make their own choices about how and where to record their work and whether it should be done individually or collaboratively. Accessing resources such as scissors, stationery and paper tends to be something that is done for children as they move further up through the school – we strongly recommend that children of whatever age take responsibility for ensuring they have the resources they need and that teachers continue to foster independence.

The starting point at James Dixon Primary School when planning a topic was that, regardless of the theme, the overarching requirement was that it must be fun and involve practical, experiential learning that drew as far as possible on resources within the local environment. When planning activities, they would start by considering what was available to support learning within the school and school grounds; next they would move to the immediate local area, then further afield possibly using public transport and sourcing visitors to support in other words, finding as many opportunities as possible to contextualise the knowledge and skills which were relevant to this topic. Staff realised that every school has its own unique environment and 'teachers actively need to seek resources to support any topic, asking themselves– what is special about us? Was our town ever invaded? Did we have an important role in World War 2? How is the name of our village derived – does it have Roman, Anglo- Saxon or Viking origins? All these questions will provide information about the immediate and wider environment – which will contribute to children's understanding of their place in their local community.

Fred gave an example of how staff at James Dixon used the environment when planning a topic on Romans for Year 3. Having looked at some artefacts which the school already had, children then went to the local park which has some architectural remains, including Roman steps. Children were taught geography skills, including visual mapping, co-ordinates, and compass directions. Another visit, a little further afield, was to a Roman villa which introduced children to an example of an architectural dig. Having experienced a real architectural dig, staff then organised an architectural dig in the school grounds which children thoroughly enjoyed. This led on to them recording their work in a variety of ways including artefact timelines, developing questions around the artefacts and writing newspaper reports, recounts and diaries. Fred made the point that it was necessary to teach both knowledge and skills, but in order to embed the skills it was important to apply them in a real-life situation such as the archaeological dig. You could give children a set of illustrations about the Romans and ask them to formulate questions in the classroom but this approach was more meaningful and memorable. Practical experiential learning helps consolidate and contextualise learning.

Summary

The key principles of implementing a play-based curriculum in Year 1 can be transferred as children move up the school. Surely the purpose of school is to provide inspirational educational experiences which breed inquisitive learners, who are capable and socially confident and develop into fully functional global citizens. Putting learning into context, so it makes sense, making the most of the outdoor learning opportunities available, including the immediate and wider local environments and linking topics to high-quality texts are all key elements in creating learners who demonstrate resilience, curiosity and the ability to develop their own ideas, who can make links between ideas and develop their own strategies for working things out.

REFLECTION

To what extent are the elements described above present in children's experiences in different age groups in your school?

References

Blake, Q. (1998) *The Green Ship*. London: Random House Children's Books.
Grill, W. (2014) *Shackleton's Journey*. London: Flying Eye Books.
James Dixon Primary School website (2020), Available at https://www.jamesdixon.bromley.sch.uk (Accessed 24 March 2020).
Pullman, P. (1995) *The Firework Maker's Daughter*. New York: Doubleday.
Rosen, M. (2019) *Michael Rosen's Book of Play*. London: Profile Books Ltd.

Afterword

Moving on in uncertain times

The Coronavirus pandemic, which in March 2020 led to a lockdown in the United Kingdom, has had an unprecedented effect on our world in ways that would have been unimaginable just a few months earlier. At the time of writing, schools are just starting to open up to a limited number of year groups, having been closed to all but a few children for several months. This is an incredibly challenging time for schools as they seek to rebuild relationships with children and their families at the same time as managing social distancing and organising class and year group "bubbles".

What is crucial at this time is that although there is a curriculum to deliver, schools must recognise that many children and families, as well as members of staff, will have experienced significant anxiety, trauma and bereavement and schools must find ways to address emotional needs and focus on well-being. Much of what has been familiar to young children in the classroom environment may no longer be available. Many schools are following current government advice to reduce the spread of infection by removing sand, role play areas and soft toys. However, it is important that the key principles of active learning, playing and exploring and creativity and critical thinking which we have emphasised throughout this book continue to underpin children's learning. Along with this, school leaders will need to provide opportunities to support pupils and staff who may well be experiencing mental health challenges, re-establish routines and expectations and ensure the specific needs of disadvantaged and other vulnerable pupils are recognised and addressed. As we have discussed throughout this book, children and young people often find transitions at any stage unsettling and stressful. It is almost inevitable therefore that many children and young people will experience these feelings when they return to school as lockdown is lifted. The principles we have outlined in Chapter 6, are just as relevant at the time of this pandemic as they are to transitions at other times in a child's life.

It is highly likely that the education system could well suffer further disruption in the future, especially if there is a spike in the number of Covid-19 cases or if other pandemics develop. Staff, as well as parents and carers, are likely to be anxious about their own and their children's safety. Whilst taking every precaution to ensure the physical health and safety of everyone in the school community, it is vital that school provides a calm, reassuring atmosphere which recognises the trauma many families will have experienced. Although classrooms will, in many cases, look different, it is important that children quickly re-establish routines, structures and social connectedness.

Over recent months, staff in schools have demonstrated the highest levels of commitment, empathy and hard work — keeping schools open over school holidays, including some bank holidays, for children of key workers, whilst at the same time doing their very best to keep in contact with families through regular phone calls, online learning and in some cases even delivering food parcels.

At the start of the lockdown, the government announced that all formal assessment in English primary schools during the rest of the school year 2019/20 would be cancelled and that primary school performance measures would not be published for the 2019/20 academic year. The principal purpose of these tests is to compare school against school and provide a measure of accountability. Given that the impact of this epidemic is likely to last for some years, with disadvantaged children and those from ethnic minority heritages disproportionately affected, there is now a golden opportunity for policy makers to review the relevance of these assessments at this time.

On returning to whatever the new "normal" looks like, it is to be hoped that senior leaders, along with government ministers and policy makers, recognise that the truly successful schools are those which are able to work with families rekindling children's natural thirst for learning, building resilience and providing reassurance. These are the schools most likely to produce children who are optimistic, confident in themselves and ready to move on to the next stage in their education.

Index

abstraction 29–32, 87
Academy Converter Schools 7
accountability 85, 90, 122
active learning 12, 19, *54*, 121
adjective **62**, 80
adult-child ratio (legal requirement) 92
adult-initiated play-based learning 66
adult-led activities 67–70, 98
adults **60**, 89, *91*; critical role in facilitating children's learning 10
adult support 3, 23, 27, 73
age (when starting school) 34–35
Allen Edwards PS (Stockwell) xii, 3, 99
archaeology 118–119
art and design 23, 67, *68*, 100, *108*
assemblies 22, 55, 110
assessment 76–80
Assessment is for Learning 33
attainment 2, 4, 15
attention 36, **59**
Attention Deficit Hyperactive Disorder 35

Banks, F. xii, 114
barriers to implementation 4, 5, 83–95; concern about standards 87–90; external pressures 83–85; lack of understanding 86–87; leadership 85–86; mixed-ability grouping 90; Ofsted 83–85, 94; pressures to adopt formal approach to learning 85; resources 92–93; statutory assessments 84–85, 95; teacher workload 93–94
baseline assessments 85
Beaver Green PS (Ashford, Kent) xi–xii, 10
beebot mat *68*, *108*
behaviour 3, 31, 41, 95
Bell, M. 33
Blackpool Council 37
Blake, Q.: *Green Ship* (1998) 111
book corner 25, 42, 57, 67
books 30–31, 66, *91*, 116

Bradbury, A. 90
Browning, M. 35
Bryce Clegg, A. 15
builder's tray 44, 48, 93
butterflies 58, 66

carers 18, 41, 55, 56, 97, 110, 122
carpet sessions xi, 11, 14, 15, 21, *22*, 23, *24*, 36–37, 57, **62**, 67, 95, 98, 99, 104
chalk 10, 21, 48, 57, **61**, **62**, 63, 64, 70, 79
Characteristics of Effective Learning 2, 4, 12, 19, 21, 31, 35, 38, *54*, 54–55, 95, *105*, 109, 114
child development 31–32, 38, 114; *see also* developmental stage
child-initiated learning 23, **60–62**, 98
children: develop and learn in different ways at different rates 12, 15, 18, 37–38, 47; independent entry into school 100; learning and development 86–87; most enjoyable aspects of EYFS *102–103*; need to challenge able 15; ownership of learning 70; summer-born 53, 106
Children and young people's mental health (government report, 2016–2017) 35–36
children's interests [enthusiasms] 2, 7, 9, 10, 20, 24, 31, 44, 51, 55, 57
Clarke, S. 90, 94; *Unlocking Formative Assessment* (2001) 94
classroom environment 15, 21, 55
classroom furniture 11, 13, 29, 41, *43*, **61**
classroom organisation 28, 42–45, 81
clipboards 10, 11, 26, 48
communication 19, 35, 57, *68*, *107*, *108*, 117
computers and computing 66, *68*, *91*, *108*
concentration 1, 12, 18, 19, 34, *54*, 66, 87, 94
construction play 49, 58, **60**, 67, *68*
continuing professional development 8
continuous provision 22–23, 58, **61**, 63, 64, 66, 67, 70, 73, 77, 86, 89, 92, 100, 104

cookery activity 25; vehicle for contextualising learning 115

core text 10, 22, 23, *24*, 56, 66, 67, *68*, 73, 77–78, 84, *108*, 109; classroom environment planned around *42–43*; link with learning 115–116

coronavirus pandemic 121–122

creative and critical thinking 12, 19, 38, *54*, 121

creative area 66, 87, 100, *105*

creative workshop *65*, 68

creativity 24, 27, 33, 66, 67, *105*, 121

critical friends 89–90

cross-curricular learning 14, 15, 23, 67, 80, 115; play-based approach 11

curiosity xi, 7, 30, 31, 38, 41, *54*, *91*, 95, 119

curriculum xii, 14, 83; balanced and broadly-based 86; child-centred 4, 31; holistic 73

curriculum (play-based) 2, 5, 7, 9–10, 31, 53, 73, 79, *107*, 109; furniture obstacle 13; transition to subject-based curriculum xi

curriculum (subject-based) 2, 4, 9, 15, 30, 54, 73, 86, 98, 100; application of effective-learning characteristics 19

Curriculum for Excellence (Scottish Government, 2008) 32–33

curriculum map 66, 114

dashboards 85

decision-making *54*, 86, *91*

Dee, T. 36

Denmark 36

Department for Children, Schools and Families (DCSF) 37

design (and) technology (DT) 77–78, *91*, 114–116

developmental stage xi, 2, 3, 18, 29, 32, 35, 39, 86, 95

digital skills 33

dinosaurs 56, 58, **59**, **62**, 67, 89, *91*

disabilities 99, *105*

disadvantaged children xi, 4, 7, 30–31, 50, 55, 80, 122

discovery 34–36, 56, 98

discrete subjects 23, *24*, 64, 73, 100

displays 11, 15, 20, 31, 42, 44, 56, 70, 111

Doyle, W. 34, 36

drawing 42, 55, **61**, **62**, 77, *91*, 100

early formal learning 35–36

Early Learning Goals (ELGs) 32, 104

Early Years Foundation Stage *see* EYFS

East Sussex 3, 8

echo reading 27, 57

Elder, T.E. 35

enabling environment 4, 5, 13, 17, 13, 24–26, 38, 41–51, 98, *105*, 109; Chinese New Year *45*; classroom organisation 42–45; classroom planned around core text *42–43*; disadvantaged children 50; mathematics outdoors *48–49*; outdoor learning area 46–47; owl babies *45*; rainforest investigation area *44*; recording work 50–51; role play area 46; role play café 46, *46*; three boys working together *47*

engagement 50, *54*, 55, 80, 94, 109

English 11, 30, 32, 46, 51, 53, 55, 57, *68*, 106, *108*, 114, 118; formal tests 84–85; writing genres 77–78

English lessons xi; mixture (whole-class, small-group, adult-or child-initiated) 56–57

enjoyment 2, 5, 12, 19, 29, 32, 44, *54*, 55, 85, 90, 93, 101, 102, *102–103*, 109, 118

enrichment experience 5, 14, 28, 80, 110, 117

enthusiasm xi, 3, 9, 10, 15, 20, 28, 31, 41, 114

Estonia (role model) 34–35

ethnic minority heritages 122

Eurydice: "Estonia, Early Childhood Education and Care" (2019) 35

excitement 10, 28, 41, **61**, 101

exercise books 10, 50, 57, 74, 79, 85, 86, 99, 118

expectations 2, 4, 7, 9, 20, 28–30, 32, 34, 37, 41, 46, 53, 55, **62**, 63, 73, 84, 86, 89, 90, 109, 110, 114, 117, 121

experiential learning xii, 30, 33, 116, 118, 119

exploration x, 11, 12, 15, 19, 23, 36, 38, 44, 47, 50, *54*, 57, 63, 66, 67, *68*, *79*, *91*, 98–100, *105*, *108*, 114, 115, 117, 121

external pressures 4, 5, 83–85, 94

EYFS (Early Years Foundation Stage; including "Reception" and "Year R") xi, xii, 3, 8–12, 14, 20–21, *20*, 23, 31, 36–37, 41, 51, 63, 65, 79, 89, 92, 95, 97–99; transition to Year One 4, 5, 11, 15, 18, 29, 85–86; transition to Year One (child's perspective) 97

EYFS curriculum 4; broad-based 83; play-based 11, 18; play-based (extension into Year One) 95; principles (equally relevant to older children) 18–19, 53, 55

EYFS Handbook (2018) 54

EYFS profile data 2, *20*, 76, 84, *102–103*, 109, 110; use in planning for Year One 104–105

EYFS provision: photography 51; possible extension 28

EYFS (Reception) staff 4–5, 31, 48

EYFS teachers 97, 101; liaising with Year One colleagues 25, 53

feedback xi, 14, 23, 51, 67, 70, 72, 80

fidgeting xi, 2, 64, 95

fireworks 115–116

Fisher, J.: *Interacting or Interfering?* (2016) 70–71; *Moving on to Key Stage 1* (2010) 32, 84

flexibility 9, 12–14, 28, 92, 100

focus group 22, 80

formal schooling 34, 35, 85, 95; appropriate time for introduction 113–114; later start 34–35

Foundation Phase (Wales) 33

Foundation Stage [later "EYFS", *qv*] 37

Foundation Stage (Northern Ireland) 33–34

foundation subjects 13, 29, 30, 51, 55, 66, 77–78, 114

fractions 87

free flow 10, 14, 15, *22*, 23, *24*, 24, 41, 64, 66–67, *68*, 70–72, 80, 98, 101, 110

fun xi, 56, 79, 84, 93, 103, 115, 114
fundamentals 2, 32, 41, 54, 109

geography 30–31, 51, 77–78, 87, *89*, *106*,
    110–115, 118
geometry *68*, 77, *108*
Gingerbread Man 73, 100, *108*
Good Level of Development (GLD) 4–5, 19–20,
    21, 53, 77, 104, *105*, 114
good practice 8, 13, 25, 109
grammar *24*, **62**, 77–78
Great Fire of London 117; contextualising
    learning 115
grid references 50
Grill, W.: *Shackleton's Journey* (2014) 116
guided groups 27, 28, 57, 92

Hallam, S. 90
hand-eye co-ordination 93
handwriting 21, *22*, *24*; developing physical skill
    needed 64
handwriting development 67, *69*
"having a go" 12, 19, *54*
headteachers xii, 3, 7, 9, 12, 37, 85, 86, 114
Heinesen, E. 35
history 51, 77–*78*, *91*, 114–115
HMCI 83, 84
home visits 10, 98
human resources xii, 92

imagination xii, 44, 46, *91*, 93, 100, *107*, 109
Inclusion lead 53
independent learning activities 11, 18–19, 22, 27,
    33, 44, 49, 51, 57, 67, *68*, 70, 87, 89, *91*, 92, 93,
    105, *107*, 118; *see also* free flow
insects 66
inspiration 114, 115, 118, 119
interactivity 9, 21, 22, 32, 46, 56, **62**
investigation 11–13, 19, 23, *24*, 47, 50, 67
investigation areas 42–45, 58
investigation prompts 93
investigation table 63, 66, 73–74, *74–76*, 78, 87
investment 8, 15, 38
involvement *54*, 58, 87
Istead Rise PS (Kent) xi, 46, 76

James Dixon PS (London) xii, 114; case study 116;
    core texts (link with learning) 115–116; enabling
    environments 118–119; "forest school" activities
    116–117; learning in context 114–115; learning
    outside classroom 116–117; website 117
junk modelling 44, 48, 58, 67

Kangas, J. 83–84
Kent 3, 7–9
Key Stage One xi, 2, 4, 11, 18, 29, 84, 90, 109,
    110, 116
Key Stage Two 5, 7, 29, 33, 116, 118

Key Stage Three 33
Key Stage Four 33

land 117
language skills 83, 89, 116
leadership 8, 11–12, 85–86, 113
learning: active, fun, meaningful 31, 84; context 94,
    114–115; "how" versus "what" 29–30, 84, 101
learning environment 5, 9, 28
learning objective (LO) 22, *24*, 57, 58
Learning to Learn (NI Government, 2013) 34
Let Children Play (Sahlberg and Doyle, 2019) 34, 36
library shed 50
listening 19, 36, 46, 57, **59**, *68*, *91*, 110, 115, 117
literacy skills 19, 22, *24*, 32, 34, 77–78, 85, 98
Little Red Riding Hood 73, 100
locality 30, 118
London 3, 8, 9, 114
lunchtime 13, 55, 63

magic chalk 57, 58, 61, 67
materials 25, 44, 49, 73, 74, 89, 93, 100, 116;
    everyday materials 30, 50, *68*, 77, *108*; natural
    materials *91*, 93, 95, 117
mathematical resources 58
mathematics xi, 1, 4–5, 11, 15, 20, *22*, 22–23, *24*,
    30, 34, 44, 48, 50, 51, 53, 55, 58, 63, 67, 77–*78*,
    84, 85, 89, *91*, 93, *94*, 98, 103, 104, *105*, 106,
    115, 118; formal tests 84–85; practical activity
    25, *94*; worksheet *25*
McDowall Clark, R. 2, 6, 31, 35, 39
meaningful learning 15, 29–31, 33, 76, 83, 84, 92,
    94, 100, 114, 119
medium-term plans 67, *68*, 76, 77–*79*, 80
mental health 35–36, 121
messy play 48, 67, 70, 87
minibeasts 66, *102*
mixed-ability groups or pairs 14, 62, 67, 90, 110
motivation xi, 2, 29, 30, 33, 35, 50, *54*, 59, 85, *91*,
    94, 117
motor control 21, 56, 63–64, 93, *107*
motor skills *24*, 63–65, 109
movement 21, 36, 64
moving forward (Year One and beyond) xii, 5,
    113–119; case study 116; enabling environments
    118–119; learning (in context) 114–115;
    learning (linked to core texts) 115–116; learning
    (outside classroom) 116–117; play (importance)
    113–114
music 21, *24*, 63, 64, *68*, *108*

narratives 59, 60
National Curriculum (NC) 11, 30, 33, 46, 49, 59–60,
    63–65, *68*, 73, 76, 80, 81, 86, 89, 99–100
National Education Union 90
National Foundation for Educational Research
    (NFER) 31, 36, 39, 104
Native Americans and Wild West 114, 117

negotiation 46, 51, 55, 86, *107*, 110, 116
New York 34
Northern Ireland 33–34
numeracy 34, 76–79, 85
nursery classes xii, 3, 10, 31, 89

Ofsted 7, 37, 39; *Bold Beginnings* (2017) 4, 83–85, 95, 96; research into school curriculum (three phases) 84, 96
online learning (coronavirus era) 122
open-ended questioning 10, *91*
Organisation for Economic Co-operation and Development (OECD) 34, 39
outcomes 28, 30, 63, 66, 81, 83 84, 87, 89, *91*, 95, *105*
outdoor learning area 1, 5, 9, 10, 14, 15, 18, 19, 24, 28, 41, 46–47, *48–49*, 50, 51, 55, 63, 64, 67, *68*, 80, 93, 98, 104, *105*, *107–108*, 114, 116–117, 119; "extension of classroom" 48; regret at loss of (transition to Year One) 101

painting 44, 48, 58, 64, 66, 67, 87, 100, *108*
paired activity 30, 61, 62, 67, 90, 110
parental involvement 20, 56, 73, 98, *105*, 110
parents 4, 5, 37, 41, 55, 85, 95, 97; coronavirus era 121; importance of play (lack of understanding) 34; partnership with schools 14, 20, 28; transition information 104, *105–106*
Parsons, S. 90, 96
pedagogy 4, 8, 9, 83, 90, 109, 114
peer-based learning 116–117
Peel Clothworkers School (Isle of Man) xii, 3, 50
Personal, Social, Emotional Development (PSED) 21, 36, 58, 77, 80, 83, 99, 106, *107*; "personal development" 19, 117
Pettett, V. 3, 4, 9–13; headteacher 3; senior leader 29
Phillips, D. 2, 6
phonics 21, *22*, 22, *24*, 27, 63, *105*
phonics screening check 2, 4, 30, 56–57, 84, 100
photographs 4, 66, *88*, 93; annotated 26, 51, 80
physical education (PE) *24*, 49, 64, 98
Pickhurst Infant Academy (Bromley) xii, 3, 37–38, 86; case study 92–93
pirates 110, 117; medium-term plan *78–79*
PISA (Programme for International Student Assessment) 34, 39
place names 115, 118
planning 73–76, 92
play xi; adult-initiated versus child-initiated 86–87; coronavirus era 121; importance 36, 113–114; importance (lack of parental understanding) 34; underpins learning for young children 86
playground 21, 55, 61, 63, 64, 79
playing and exploring 12, 19, *54*

play quality 10, 70
playtimes 55, 97
practice 2, 4, 5, 12, 53–81; adult-initiated activities 66, 67, 73; assessment 76–80; building on prior learning 53–54; child-initiated activities 66, 70–71; creative workshop shared area *65*; free flow 66–67; free flow (role of adult) 70–72; investigation tables 73–74, *74–76*; planning 73–76; science investigation area *74–76*; storing resources shared area *65*; summary 80–81; timetable 54–76
prediction 27, *54*, 57, 60
prior attainment 53–54
problem-solving 15, 24, 33, 34, 50, *54*, 70, *91*, *107*, *108*
professional judgement 23, 64
Public Policy Institute for Wales 33, 39
public speaking skills 46
Pullman, P. 115, 119
punctuation 62, *77–78*
pupil engagement 14, 15

quality of life 32
questionnaires 97, 101
quiet space 50
Quirk, S. 3, 4, 8, 12–13; headteacher 3; senior leader 29; Year One teaching "most challenging" 29

rationale for change 3–5, 29–39; behaviour issues (Year One) 31; child development theories 31–32; children's well-being and mental health 35–36; disadvantaged children 30–31; early formal learning 35–36; experience of Pickhurst Infant Academy 37–38; impact of age on starting school 34–35; standardised testing (impact on teaching methods) 34; teaching and learning approaches across UK 32–34; transition from Reception into Year One (research) 36–37
RE *24*, 51
reading 5, *24*, 34, 53, 56, 67, 81, 83, 104, 116; guided groups 27, 28; NC objectives 59–60; whole-class sessions 27
reading groups 57, 73
reading skills 22, 23, 87
Reception, *see* EYFS
recording work 13, 50–51
reflection 2, 4, 11, 12, 16, 38, 51, 54, 81, 90, 95, 99, 111, 119
Regis Manor Primary School 7
resilience 2, 4, 18, 54, 104, 119, 122
resources xii, 1, 8, 10, 15, 24, 25, 28, 29, 41, 44, 48, 50, 58–60, 62, 66, *68*, 70, 86, 87, 89, *91*, 92–93, 95, *105*, *107–108*, 118; case study 92–93; storing resources shared area *65*

Roberts-Holmes, G. 90, 95
Robinson, M. 31–32, 39, 64, 81
Rockmount PS (Croydon) xii, 3, 9, 51, 86, 89–90
role play 25, 48, 57, 60, *68*, 87, 89, *107*, *108*
role play area 44, 46, 58, 64, 67, 121
Romans 118–119
Rosen, M. 113, 119

Sachar, L. 114
Sahlberg, P. 34, 36, 39
sand play 49, 58, 70, 87, 89, 121
SATs 2, 4, 84, 100
scaffolding 10, 11, 62
Scherer, L. 90, 96
school gates 55, 97
school governors 3, 5, 85
school improvement adviser 3, 8
school leaders 2–5, 85, 95, 117, 121
science *24*, 30, 34, 49, 50, 64, *68*, 77–78, 89, *91*, 98, *108*, 115, 118; NC requirements 76
science investigation area *74–76*
Scotland 32–33
sea 30–31
self-esteem 35, 117
self-registration 21, *22*, *24*, 56
senior leaders 11, 14, 31, 38, 51, 55, 76, 86, 89–90, 118; coronavirus era 122
Sharp, C. 36, 39
Sievertson, H. 36, 39
sitting still 31, 36
skill progression 15, 89, 92
small-group teaching 14, 15, 58, 60–63, 79, 87, 92, 100, 117
small peg boards 21, 64, *107*
small-world play 25, 45, 57, 58, 60, 67, *68*, 89, 93, *107*, *108*; prompt sheet 89, *90–91*
social skills 36, *68*, 89
special educational needs 99
Special Educational Needs Co-ordinator (SENDCo) 19, 53, *105*
spelling 60, 77–78
Spielman, A. 84, 96
spoken language 46, 59, *68*, *91*, *108*
staff 7, 10, 13–15, 29
staffing and staffing ratios 13, 28, 55, 63, 81
standards 87–91; case study 89–90; small world prompt sheet *91*
statutory assessments 84–85, 95
Statutory Framework for EYFS (Department for Education, 2018) 2, 6, 12, 109, 111
Stipek, D. 2, 6
story time 20, *22*, *24*, 57, 73
stress 36, 90, 121
Superheroes 77, 94
Supertato 1, 77
support staff 7, 8, 12, 13, 101
Sutton Trust 90, 96

Swale Academies Trust (2010–) xi–xii, 2–5, 7, 8, 16, 46, 101–102, 113, 114; advisory headteachers 8; consistent approach 12–14; developing play-based learning in Year One 11–12; Director of Primaries 9, 11–12; disseminating effective practice 9–10; growth 8, 9, 15; key feature 8; origins 3, 5, 7–16; practical issues 13–14; Primary Improvement Team 8, 12; priority 8; senior leadership 8–10; successes and challenges 14–15; training activities 13, 15, 17–28, 31, 38; website 8; Year One provision (guidance document) 13, 17–28; youngest children (getting it right) 8–9

table-based work 98
TACTYC: *Bald Beginnings!* (2017) 83, 96
teacher-led activities 10, 23, 27, 98
teachers xi, 1–5, 7, 8, 11–13, 20, 28, 36; definition 3; professional autonomy required 84; Year One "buddied" with EYFS 38
teacher workload 93–94
teaching assistants (TAs) 3, 5, 8, 13, 20, 23, 59, 63, 67, 81, 92, 98, *103*, 109; Year One-EYFS liaison 109
teaching quality 8, 29
teaching to test (league table outcomes) 84
testing 34, 36, 84
Thomson, W.: *Chalk* (2010) 57–58, 67, 81
threading 21, 64, *107*
Three Little Pigs 57, 67, *68*, 73, 100
time 4, 63, 93
timetables 4, 5, 13, 21, *22*, *24*, 27, 30, 98; Year One 53–73
toilet use 55, 97, 102
traditional tales 100, 117
training programme (one-day) for EYFS and Year One staff 17–28; afternoon session 23; aims 17; effective learning (characteristics) 19; effective transition (Year R to Year One) 20; enabling environments 24–26; good level of development 19–20; mid-September to Term Five 21; points for consideration 22–23, 25–26, 28; principles into practice 18–19; rationale 18; September ("new month, unique chapter") 20–21; shared understanding 17; terms five and six 27–28; timetables *22*, *24*, 27
transition action plan 105, *105–106*, 111
transition day 106, 109
transitions 4–5, 97–111; arrangements within school 109–110; children's perspectives 95, 102–104, *102–103*; coronavirus era 121; curriculum coverage 99–100; familiarity of routines 99–100 (case study 97); getting to know children 98–99; information for parents *107–108*, 109; parental concerns 98; questionnaire for parents 101; teachers" viewpoints 97–99; use of EYFS profile data to plan for Year One 104–105; Westland PS 104
transition week 101, 109, 110

trauma (coronavirus era) 121, 122
tuff spots 48, 50, *68*, *108*
tweezer use 21, 56, 63, 64, 93, 107
two-form entry school 13–14, 81

UN Convention on Rights of Child 32
understanding (Early Learning Goal) 92
United Kingdom 30, 32–34, 38, *79*, 115, 121
United States 34

vocabulary 57, 59, 61–62, *68*, 69, 87, *89*, 116;
    geographical 30; lists of words on walls and
    vocabulary mats 1; mathematical 50; word banks
    62; wow words 44, 77–*78*, 80
vulnerable children 97, 99, *105*, 121

Wales 33
water play 1, 50, 55, 58, 70, 87
well-being 35–36, 37, 121
Westlands Primary School (Sittingbourne) xi–xii,
    3, 9–10, 12, 17, 51; new headteacher 7–8;
    play-based curriculum (Year One) 11
Westlands Secondary School 7
whiteboard 11, 25, 56, 59, 61, 64; interactive 21,
    56, 62
whole-class sessions 21, 30, 59–63, 80, 91, 100
Wilson, M. xi, 7–8, 11–12
wonder 14, 41, 81
Wood, J. xi, 10
worksheets 3, 4, 25, *25*, 29, 30, 63, 79, 93, 95
workshop area 25, 64, 67, 87, 89
writing 4, 5, 10, *24*, 37, 50, 51, 53, 55, 57, 62, 84,
    104, 109, 114, 116; NC objectives 60; outdoors
    27; for pleasure *26*; table not always needed 26;
    wrist-bone development 32, 64
writing area 44, 70
writing groups 73

writing opportunities 48, *69*, *107*
writing skills 11, 22, 23, 27, 67, 80; improvement
    85, *88*, 89
writing table: "essential in Year One" 25

Year R, *see* EYFS
Year One xi, xii, 1–5, 11, 33, 41, 49–51, 73, 87;
    distinct lack of resources for play 29; phonics
    screening check 2, 4, 30, 56, 84, 100; putting
    ideas into practice 53–80; teaching challenges 18;
    topic-planning 55; transition from EYFS 11–12,
    28, 51; transition to Year Two 4, 14, 27–28
Year One classrooms: resources 92–93; should
    resemble EYFS classrooms 109
Year One curriculum 18, 81, 109; "Let Me Be
    Five" (*cri de cœur*) x; purpose of this book 2, 5;
    should be aligned with that of EYFS (rather
    than vice-versa) 83–84
Year One provision 12–13, 17–28
Year One staff 4–5, 28, 48
Year One teachers 67, 76–79, 97–110;
    interpretation of EYFS data 53; liaison with
    EYFS counterparts 55, 109
Year One timetable 54–73; afternoon sessions
    67–69; break time 58; end of morning
    (recapitulation) 63; lunchtime 63–64; sequence
    of learning 58, 59–62; Session One-early
    morning work 56; Session Two-phonics 56;
    Session Three-English 56–58; Session Four-
    mathematics 58–63; Session Five 63–64; Session
    Six 64–73; Session Seven-class story time 73;
    end of day 73
Year Two 4, 18, 32, 33, 74, 85, 98, 116; SATs 100
Year Three 116
Year Four 1, 41, 85
Year Five 41
Year Six 5, 85